LAW
BASICS
Student Study Guides

HUMAN RIGHTS

THIRD EDITION

LAW
BASICS
Student Study Guides

HUMAN RIGHTS

THIRD EDITION

By

Alastair N Brown
*LLB, PhD, Advocate, Sheriff of Tayside,
Central and Fife at Dundee*

W. GREEN

THOMSON REUTERS

First edition published in 2000
Second edition published in 2005
Third edition published in 2014

Published in 2014 by W. Green, 21 Alva Street
Edinburgh EH2 4PS
Part of Thomson Reuters (Professional) UK Limited
(Registered in England & Wales, Company No 1679046. Registered
Office and address for service: Aldgate House, 33 Aldgate High Street,
London EC3N 1DL)

www.wgreen.co.uk

Typeset by Alex Nashed at W. Green, Edinburgh
Printed in Great Britain by CPI Group (UK) Ltd,
Croydon, CR0 4YY.

No natural forests were destroyed to make this product;
only farmed timber was used and replanted.

A CIP catalogue record of this book is available from the British Library.

ISBN 978-0-414-3352-8

Thomson Reuters and the Thomson Reuters logo are
trademarks of Thomson Reuters.

© Thomson Reuters (Professional) UK Limited 2014

- 2 FEB 2018

DEDICATION

*For my mother, Evelyn Brown, and in memory of my father,
Kenneth Brown.*

CONTENTS

TABLE OF CASES

1. INTRODUCTION

This book is about human rights law as it applies in Scotland. That means **1–01** that although international human rights law is a very wide field indeed, almost everything written in this book is concerned with the European Convention on Human Rights and Fundamental Freedoms 1950 ("ECHR"). The Charter of Fundamental Rights of the European Union (which has had little practical effect) applies where a Member State is implementing EU law but, otherwise, human rights treaties are only available for the use of national courts in the UK where the language of statute is ambiguous and one of the possible meanings is consistent with a treaty to which the UK is party while other possible meanings are not. In such a case, the treaty can be used as an aid to interpretation, on the presumption that Parliament intends to legislate in conformity with the UK's international obligations (*Salomon v Commissioners of Customs and Excise* (1967); *T Petitioner* (1997)). So far as ECHR is concerned, however, the effect of the Human Rights Act 1998 ("HRA") is to incorporate the treaty into national law and require the courts to take it into account irrespective of any statutory ambiguity. In Ch.2 we shall look at how it does that.

The remaining chapters of the book outline each of the rights guaranteed by States under ECHR and enforceable in Scotland (and the rest of the UK) as a result of the HRA. The aim is to give the reader a good basic understanding of the principles. It is, however, important to read the cases themselves. The way in which the European Court of Human Rights ("the Strasbourg Court" or "the Court", except where the context indicates otherwise) reasons is understood most easily by reading its judgements, which are available at its website, *http://www.echr.coe.int*. It is also important to understand that it is not the intention, in a LawBasics text, to give an exhaustive account of UK or even just Scots cases on human rights law. The cases selected for inclusion in this book are selected because they articulate or exemplify principles.

This chapter introduces ECHR, the Strasbourg Court and the general principles that apply to the application and interpretation of ECHR.

ECHR
The place of ECHR in international human rights law
ECHR represents a small part of international human rights law. As a whole, international human rights law consists of a wide range of texts, **1–02** some binding and others merely recommendations. Some of those instruments are global, like the International Covenant on Civil and Political Rights 1976. Others (such as ECHR itself) are regional, in that they apply only in a particular part of the world. The American Convention on Human Rights 1969 and the African Charter on Human and Peoples Rights 1981 are other examples.

1

Some international human rights instruments are general in that they deal with a range of rights. Others, such as the European Convention for the Prevention of Torture and Inhuman or Degrading Treatment or Punishment 1987, deal with specific types of human rights violations. Others, such as the UN Convention on the Rights of the Child 1989, address the needs of particular sections of humanity.

It is common to treat international human rights law in three "generations":

(1) Civil and political rights. This includes ECHR and is, accordingly, the only "generation" dealt with in this book.
(2) Economic, social and cultural rights. Examples include rights to an adequate standard of living, to food, clothing and housing and to take part in the cultural life of the community.
(3) Collective or peoples' rights. Examples include the right to development and the right of colonised peoples to freedom.

The development of ECHR

1–03 ECHR was the first fully developed human rights treaty and it has exercised significant influence on other first generation human rights treaties as well as on many of the national constitutions drafted in the second half of the 20th century. Its origins can be traced beyond Europe, to the United Nations. For practical purposes, the starting point is the Charter of the United Nations, signed on June 26, 1945. The preamble states that the peoples of the United Nations were determined

> "to reaffirm faith in fundamental human rights, in the dignity and worth of the human person, in the equal rights of men and women".

Article 1.3 states that one of the purposes of the UN is:

> "To achieve international co-operation in solving international problems of an economic, social, cultural or humanitarian character, and *in promoting and encouraging respect for human rights and for fundamental freedoms* without distinction as to race, sex, language or religion" [emphasis added].

Work on this within the framework of the UN proceeded relatively slowly. Meanwhile, the Council of Europe was established in May 1949. (The Council of Europe is an entirely separate body from the European Union, with a much wider membership and an entirely different role. These bodies must not be confused.)

A "Charter of Human Rights" had been contemplated specifically in the process which led to the establishment of the Council of Europe and Article 1.b of the Statute of the Council of Europe committed the Member States to, amongst other things, "the maintenance and further realisation of human rights and fundamental freedoms".

Article 3 of the Statute provided:

> "Every Member ... must accept the principles of the rule of law and of the enjoyment by all persons within its jurisdiction of human rights and fundamental freedoms."

In furtherance of these aspirations, the Council of Europe set up a committee of experts to prepare what was to become ECHR. It is clearly recorded in government papers from the time that the first Part of ECHR, which contains the substantive rights, was based very closely indeed on texts proposed by the UK that were considered to be consistent with the existing state of English law. ECHR was signed at Rome on November 4, 1950 and entered into force on September 3, 1953.

THE CONVENTION RIGHTS

The rights

ECHR sets out a number of rights. This book deals with those which are **1–04** incorporated into UK law by the HRA. They are:
- Article 2: The right to life.
- Article 3: The right not to be subjected to torture or to inhuman or degrading treatment or punishment.
- Article 4: The right not to be held in slavery or to be required to perform forced labour.
- Article 5: The right to liberty and security of person.
- Article 6: The right to a fair hearing.
- Article 7: The right not to be subjected to retrospective criminalisation.
- Article 8: The right to respect for private and family life, home and correspondence.
- Article 9: The right to freedom of thought, conscience and religion.
- Article 10: The right to freedom of expression.
- Article 11: The right to freedom of assembly and association.
- Article 12: The right to marry and found a family.
- Article 14: The right not to be subject to discrimination in the enjoyment of the other Convention rights.

There are in addition a number of Protocols to the Convention. The UK is not party to all of those Protocols, but the following rights in Protocols are incorporated by the HRA:
- Protocol 1, Article 1: The right to peaceful enjoyment of possessions.
- Protocol 1, Article 2: The right to education.
- Protocol 1, Article 3: The right to free elections.
- Protocol 13: The abolition of the death penalty.

In this book, as in the HRA, the expression "the Convention rights" is used to refer to these rights

Positive obligations

1–05 In general, the Convention rights are couched in negative terms. States undertake to refrain from doing certain things. But the Court has developed the concept of the "positive obligation". That means that although some of the provisions of the Convention are couched in negative language, they actually require the State to promote the enjoyment of the right concerned and not merely to refrain from interfering with it.

So, for example, *McCann v UK* (1995) and *Kaya v Turkey* (1999) made it clear that the right to life, guaranteed by art.2, means that in a case where it is alleged or established that the right has been breached by police or security services the state is under a positive obligation to conduct a thorough, impartial and effective investigation and that the uncritical acceptance by the public prosecutor of police reports will fall far short of discharging that obligation.

Johnston v Ireland (1987) provides a helpful example from a different context. That case concerned, amongst other things, the position of the illegitimate child in Irish law. The Strasbourg Court held that, although art.8 has as its essential object the protection of the individual against arbitrary interference by the public authorities with her private or family life, there may in addition be positive obligations inherent in an effective "respect" for family life. In particular, the state had an obligation to put in place arrangements so that the disabilities suffered by an illegitimate child (especially as regards her inheritance rights) were removed so as to respect her family relationship with her father.

THE EUROPEAN COURT OF HUMAN RIGHTS

The original arrangements

1–06 In its original form, ECHR established two organs for the enforcement of the rights which it guarantees, these being the European Commission of Human Rights ("the Commission") and the Strasbourg Court. Protocol 11 abolished the Commission and reconstructed the Court with effect from November 1998, essentially because the structures could not cope with the large and increasing caseload. The Commission remained in being until November 1999 to deal with cases which were "on its books" in November 1998. The Court and the Commission are and were based in Strasbourg, where the Council of Europe also has its seat.

The Commission could receive applications from any person claiming to be the victim of a violation of a Convention right by one of the states party to ECHR which had made a declaration that it recognised the competence of the Commission to receive such applications. The UK recognised that competence with effect from January 1966. From this procedure is derived the term used for a person who asks the Court to consider a case. They are called "the applicant".

Having received an application, the Commission required first to consider its admissibility. Amongst a number of grounds on which the Commission could find an application inadmissible, the one that is of most practical importance for us is that that dealt with the application which was held to be manifestly ill-founded. Commission decisions on this ground often contain reasoning which is helpful in interpreting the Convention.

The Strasbourg Court has as many judges as there are parties to ECHR. **1–07** Each judge is elected for six years. The Court sits in Committees of three judges, in Chambers of seven judges and in a Grand Chamber of 17 judges. Cases go first to a Committee and that Committee is entitled, by unanimous vote, to declare that a given application is inadmissible, provided that further examination of the case is not necessary. The criteria are essentially those previously applied by the Commission. Some further amendments to the detail of this are made by Protocol 14 but these are largely technical and need not be considered here. That said, it is worth noting that the Protocol introduces a rule that an application is inadmissible if the applicant has not suffered a "significant disadvantage". Much the same point was made by Poole, J. in *R (on the application of M and Leon La Rose) v Commissioner of Police for the Metropolis* (2001) when he commented that ECHR does not exist to be invoked when the deprivation of a right is theoretical and illusory.

Where the Committee is unable to declare that an application is inadmissible a decision is taken on the admissibility and the merits of the application by a Chamber. Where an application is held to be admissible, the Court attempts to secure a "friendly settlement". If that cannot be achieved, it proceeds to decide the case. Within three months of the decision of the Chamber a party can, in exceptional circumstances, request that the matter be referred to a Grand Chamber. A panel of five judges of the Grand Chamber will consider whether to grant that request. Where a case raises a serious question affecting the interpretation of the Convention, the Chamber may itself relinquish jurisdiction in favour of the Grand Chamber.

Where the Court finds that there has been a breach of the Convention and that the internal law of the state concerned allows only partial reparation for that, it is required to "afford just satisfaction" to the injured party. The Court has sometimes tended to hold that its decision that there has been a breach is sufficient satisfaction. But where there is a demonstrable financial loss the Court is prepared to order the state to pay compensation. In *Saunders v UK* (1996), having held that the applicant had been convicted and imprisoned after a trial that had been rendered unfair by the way in which the prosecution had used answers extracted from the applicant under compulsory powers which were not intended for use in a trial, the Court held that the finding of a violation constituted sufficient just satisfaction. By contrast, in *Pine Valley Developments Ltd v Ireland* (1994), where the Court held that the applicants had been discriminated against in relation to planning legislation, to their quantifiable financial loss, a financial award was made.

The classes of case law

1–08 The classes of case law which arise out of all of this, and which are relevant to s.2 of the HRA (discussed in Ch.2) are as follows:

- *Judgement.* Final determination of a case by the Strasbourg Court.
- *Decision of the European Court of Human Rights.* A decision by a Chamber as to admissibility.
- *Declaration.* A declaration by a Committee of the Court that an application is inadmissible.
- *Advisory opinion.* Advisory opinions may be given by the Court in terms of art.47, when the Committee of Ministers request advice as to the interpretation of the Convention or its Protocols.
- *Opinion of the Commission.* The opinion the Commission expressed as to whether or not there had been a breach of the Convention, once the application had been found to be admissible and attempts to arrive at a friendly settlement had failed.
- *Decision of the Commission.* A Commission decision on the admissibility of the application.
- *Decision of the Committee of Ministers.* A decision taken by the Committee of Ministers of the Council of Europe in cases in which the Commission had given its opinion on whether or not there had been a breach but which had not been referred to the Court.

The Court has also developed what it calls its "pilot-judgment" procedure as a means of dealing with large groups of identical cases that derive from the same underlying problem. When the court receives a significant number of applications deriving from the same root cause, it may select one or more for priority treatment. In dealing with the selected case or cases, it will seek to achieve a solution that extends beyond the particular case or cases, so as to cover all similar cases that raise the same issue. The other, related, cases are adjourned to give the national authorities time to take any steps necessary to remedy any dysfunction identified in national law. The first such case was *Bronowski v Poland* (2004). Where the state takes effective measures (including making appropriate compensation) the other cases are struck out.

INTERPRETATION OF THE CONVENTION

Introduction

1–09 The Convention is not a domestic statute and the European Court of Human Rights is not a domestic court. The Convention is a treaty and the Strasbourg Court is an international tribunal tasked with the interpretation of that treaty. The Court itself summarised its task in this way:

"The Convention and the Protocol, which relate to matters normally falling within the domestic legal order of the Contracting States, are international instruments whose main purpose is to lay down certain international standards to be observed by the Contracting States in their relations with persons under their jurisdiction. The jurisdiction of the Court extends to all cases concerning the interpretation and application of those instruments" (*Belgian Linguistic Case (No.1)* (1979–1980)).

That means that the approach the Court takes to the interpretation of the Convention is governed by international law and not by the principles of domestic statutory interpretation.

Detailed rules for the interpretation of treaties are provided by the Vienna Convention on the Interpretation of Treaties 1969. Those are the basis of the rules which are applied by the Court.

A number of principles are usually said to apply to the interpretation of ECHR, though there is very substantial overlap between them. They are as follows:

* no *quatrième* instance;
* margin of appreciation;
* autonomous meaning;
* interpretation in good faith and in accordance with ordinary meaning;
* object and purpose;
* effective interpretation;
* use of *travaux prépartatoires*; and
* dynamic or evolutive interpretation; reliance on European national law standards.

No *quatrième* instance

As we have seen, the Court is an international tribunal tasked with the **1–10** interpretation of a treaty. It is not a court of further appeal from national courts. One should never speak of "appealing to Strasbourg". The Court itself has consistently made a distinction between its own province and that of the national authorities. It says that it is not a court of "*quatrième* instance"—that is, it will treat the national court's interpretation of national laws as conclusive. It is concerned only with the question whether the state has fulfilled its obligations in terms of the Convention. In *Saunders v United Kingdom* (1996), for example, the Court held that the applicant's trial had been unfair but said in terms that it could not comment on whether the outcome of that trial had been correct or not. On that basis, it was held in *Locabail (UK) Ltd v Waldorf Investment Corporation (No.4)* (2000) that a stay of proceedings in an English court pending an application to Strasbourg would not be granted because the outcome in Strasbourg would not affect the outcome of the English proceedings.

Margin of appreciation

It will also be helpful to understand the concept of the margin of **1–11** appreciation, a principle most clearly articulated in *Handyside v UK* (1979–1980), in which the Court said:

> "By reason of their direct and continuous contact with the vital forces of their countries, state authorities are in principle in a better position than the international judge to give an opinion on the exact content of those requirements ... "

In that case, the requirements concerned were those relating to the protection of public morals. What the Court was doing was refusing to intervene where they thought that the question of what was necessary in a democratic society was best decided by the national authorities in that society. However, they went on to say that art.10.2, which deals with freedom of expression and with which they were concerned in that case, does not give the contracting states

> "an unlimited margin of appreciation. The Court, which ... is responsible for ensuring the observance of those States' engagements, is empowered to give the final ruling on whether a restriction ... is reconcilable with freedom of expression as protected by Article 10".

To put it another way, the outer limits of what is acceptable are established by the Convention and policed by the Court. Within those limits, Member States may select their own boundaries according to national conditions and perceptions. Whilst the judges of the Court might not agree that what a state has done is entirely appropriate, provided it does not go outside the limits of the Convention, in principle the Court will not interfere. (There have, however, been concerns expressed recently that the Court does not always allow a sufficient margin of appreciation.)

It should also be said that the width of the margin of appreciation varies from article to article. For example, in art.10 there is a wide margin of appreciation, but in art.3, which prohibits torture and inhuman or degrading treatment, there is virtually none. It is one thing to say that it is for individual states to decide—within broad limits—what aspects of public morality are to be restricted by the use of criminal sanctions that limit freedom of expression. It would be quite another to say that it is for individual states to decide whether or not to torture people.

Margin of appreciation is not a principle applied as such by the UK courts. However, in *Brown v Stott* (2001), Lord Bingham of Cornhill stated:

> "Judicial recognition and assertion of the human rights defined in the Convention is not a substitute for the processes of democratic government but a complement to them. While a national court does not accord the margin of appreciation recognised by the European Court as a supra-national court, it will give weight to the decisions of a representative legislature and a democratic government within the discretionary area of judgement accorded to those bodies."

Autonomous meaning

When the Convention uses a technical term it does not necessarily use it in **1–12** the same way as any given national legal system. Some terms are used by many national legal systems and their precise meanings vary from national system to national system. For example, the expression "criminal charge" is used in the Convention and also by most, if not all, legal systems; but the scope of the expression varies from system to system. Fixed penalties, for example, are characterised as criminal matters in some systems and as administrative in others. The need for consistency in meaning has led the Strasbourg Court to develop its own definitions of such words. This is the principle of "autonomous meaning". Its practical result is that, when reading cases from the Court, one must be careful not to assume that words that have a particular technical meaning in one's own legal system are necessarily used in precisely the same way by the Court.

The point was underlined by the Court of Appeal in *Re A (Children) (Conjoined Twins: Medical Treatment) (No.1)* (2002) when it pointed out that ECHR is to be construed as an autonomous text, without regard to any special rules of national law. One might say that national law must be understood in light of ECHR (as s.3 of the HRA specifically requires). However, although common European practice is a tool for interpreting ECHR (as explained at para.1–17 below), individual national rules are not.

Interpretation in good faith and in accordance with ordinary meaning

Article 31 of the 1969 Vienna Convention provides that **1–13**

> "a treaty shall be interpreted in good faith in accordance with the ordinary meaning to be given to the terms of the treaty in their context and in the light of its object and purpose".

An early example of the application of the "ordinary meaning" principle is to be found in *Luedicke, Belkacem and Koc v Federal Republic of Germany* (1979–1980). Each of the applicants was a foreign national with limited command of German who had been prosecuted and convicted of an offence in Germany and ordered to pay the costs of the proceedings, including the interpretation costs. Each applied to the Commission on the basis that the requirement to pay for the interpreter to whose services the Convention entitled them constituted a breach of art.6.3(e).

The Court held that in interpreting art.6.3(e) it would be guided by the Vienna Convention on the Law of Treaties 1969. In both French and English (the Court's two official languages) the terms "gratuitement" and "free", which art.6.3(e) uses to describe the basis on which the interpreter's services are to be provided, are unqualified, denoting a once and for all exemption or exoneration. It had to be determined whether context and object and purpose negated that literal interpretation. To read the article as allowing the domestic court to require a person who has been convicted to meet interpretation costs would be to limit art.6.3(e) in time and in practice to deny its benefit to a person who is eventually convicted. This might have implications for fair trial. The ordinary meaning of "gratuitement" and "free" is not contradicted by context or by object and purpose and the requirement to pay interpretation costs therefore amounted to a breach of the Convention.

The same point can be illustrated from *Golder v United Kingdom* (1979–1980), in which the Court was concerned with art.6.1 of the Convention. So far as relevant, that provides that:

> "In the determination of his civil rights and obligations or of any criminal charge against him, everyone is entitled to a fair and public hearing in a reasonable time by an independent and impartial tribunal established by law ... "

The facts in *Golder* were that a prisoner wished to sue a prison officer for libel in respect of a statement he made which alleged that the prisoner had participated in riot. As a result of that statement, sundry privileges were stopped, though formal disciplinary action was not taken against the prisoner. He was therefore unable to contest the allegation except by recourse to the civil courts. The prison governor stopped his letter to his solicitor, so preventing him from taking civil action. The Court held that art.6 means what it says—everyone is entitled to a hearing to determine his civil rights. The UK Government had argued that art.6 only applies where proceedings have already been commenced; in other words, that if there was a hearing it had to be fair but that there was no right to a hearing as such. The Court held that construction to be incorrect because it limited the words of the Convention in a way not justified by their ordinary meanings. By the action of the governor in stopping the letter, the applicant had been denied his right to a hearing to determine his civil rights, so that there was a breach of art.6.

Object and purpose
1–14 *Golder* (1979–1980) helps us with object and purpose as an interpretative tool as well. The Strasbourg Court took into account the fact that the preamble to ECHR emphasises the "rule of law" as part of the object and purpose of the Convention and considered that the maintenance of the rule of law cannot be maintained if some classes of potential litigant are denied access to the courts. This consideration helped the Court to conclude that the UK was wrong in its argument that art.6.1 did not give a right to a hearing as such.

Effective interpretation
1–15 The next principle is that of effective interpretation. This may best be illustrated by *Artico v Italy* (1981). In that case, the applicant had been convicted of fraud and obtained the appointment of a legal aid lawyer for his appeal. From the outset, that lawyer refused to act (on account of other commitments and the state of his health) and the applicant was, therefore, unrepresented at his appeal, which he lost.

Article 6.3(c) entitles everyone charged with a criminal offence to defend themselves in person or through legal assistance of their own choosing or, if they have not sufficient means to pay for legal assistance, to be given it free when the interests of justice so require. The Italian Government argued that its responsibilities were fully discharged when the lawyer had been appointed but the Court was not prepared to accept that argument. It said that

> "the Convention is intended to guarantee not rights that are theoretical or illusory but rights that are practical and effective ... mere nomination does not ensure effective assistance".

It held that there had been a breach of the Convention.

Use of *travaux préparatatoires*

It is legitimate in treaty interpretation to refer to the record of the 1–16 discussions that led to the treaty. The Court sometimes uses this tool of interpretation but it does so only occasionally. An example is to be found in *Hirst v United Kingdom* (2005), in which the Court considered the UK's prohibition on prisoners voting. The Convention right that was in issue was to be found in art.3 of Protocol 1, which embodies an undertaking by state parties to "hold free elections ... under conditions which will ensure the free expression of the opinion of the people in the choice of the legislature". Whilst reaffirming that margin of appreciation in this area is wide, the Court noted from the record of the preparatory work that the "unique phrasing" of the provision (in the sense that it is expressed as an undertaking rather than as the protection of a particular right) was intended to give greater solemnity to the contracting states' commitment and to emphasise that this was an area where they were required to take positive measures as opposed to merely refraining from interference. In the particular case, the Court found that the blanket ban was disproportionate and constituted a breach of the right. (As a general rule, blanket bans struggle to pass the test of proportionality that applies to many of the rights in the Convention. As in domestic judicial review, what is often required is meaningful consideration of the actual circumstances of the particular case.)

Dynamic or evolutive interpretation; reliance on European national law standards

Dynamic or evolutive interpretation and reliance on European national law 1–17 standards are very closely related. The basic principle was stated in *Tyrer v United Kingdom* (1979–1980), in which the Court said that the Convention is "a living instrument which ... must be interpreted in the light of present day conditions".

On that basis, it held that judicial corporal punishment could no longer be regarded as consistent with the art.3 prohibition on degrading punishment. However, there are limits to the principle of evolutive interpretation. In particular, it does not extend to creating a right not in the

Convention in the first place (*Johnston v Ireland* (1986)).

European national law standards are important to the Court in determining how to apply the principle of evolutive interpretation. If there is a developed, or clearly developing, consensus amongst Council of Europe Member States about what is or is not acceptable conduct, this will inform the approach of the Court. Sometimes comparative law techniques are applied to discover if there is such a consensus and, if so, what its content is. In other cases, such consensus may be identified from the existence of other, widely ratified, Council of Europe Conventions.

In *Tyrer v United Kingdom* (1979–1980), a comparative law approach permitted the Court to hold that there was an identifiable move away from judicial corporal punishment throughout Europe. More recently, in *Selmouni v France* (2000) the Court used this approach to hold that police mistreatment of the applicant, of a sort that would previously have been regarded as inhuman and degrading treatment, could now be regarded as torture.

2. HUMAN RIGHTS ACT 1998

INTRODUCTION

According to the White Paper, *Rights Brought Home*, which was published **2–01** at the beginning of the legislative process for the Human Rights Act 1998 ("HRA")

> "the essential feature of the Human Rights Bill is that the United Kingdom will not be bound to give effect to the Convention rights merely as a matter of international law, but will also give them further effect directly in our domestic law".

In Scotland, that is also the effect of s.57(2) of the Scotland Act 1998, which operates under substantial reference to the HRA and which (as amended) provides that:

> "A member of the Scottish Government has no power to make any subordinate legislation, or to do any other act, so far as the legislation or act is incompatible with any of the Convention rights or with EU law."

Lord Justice-General Rodger said, in *HM Advocate v Montgomery and Coulter* (1999) that

> "it would be wrong ... to see the rights under the European Convention as somehow forming a wholly separate stream in our law; in truth they soak through and permeate the areas of our law in which they apply".

That comment is as applicable to the effect of the HRA as to the effect of s.57(2) of the Scotland Act. In *Begum v Tower Hamlets LBC* (2002), Lord Justice Laws explained that the task of the court is

> "not simply to add on the Strasbourg learning to the corpus of English law as if it were a compulsory adjunct taken from an alien source, but to develop a municipal law of human rights by the incremental method of the common law, case by case, taking account of the Strasbourg jurisprudence as the HRA s.2 enjoins us to do".

HUMAN RIGHTS ACT 1998 SECTION 6(1)

Section 6(1) of the Human Rights Act is the pivotal provision in that Act. **2–02** It provides that "it is unlawful for a public authority to act in a way which is incompatible with a Convention right".

There are three things to be understood in this. They are:

- the meaning of "public authority";
- the meaning of "act"; and
- the effect of an act being unlawful in terms of the section.

Public authority

2–03 Section 6(3) provides that the expression "public authority" includes a court or tribunal and also "any person certain of whose functions are functions of a public nature". "Court" is not further defined but s.21(1) tells us that "tribunal" means "any tribunal in which legal proceedings may be brought". In *Douglas v Hello! Ltd* (2001), Lord Justice Keane noted that one effect of this is arguably to include the court's activity in interpreting and developing the common law, even where no public authority is party to the litigation.

The second part of the definition of a public authority is "any person certain of whose functions are functions of a public nature". At its core, this is straightforward enough. It plainly covers organisations such as the police, the fire service, NHS trusts, local authorities and the Procurator Fiscal Service. Any number of other bodies that are obviously public could be identified. The more difficult questions are likely to arise at the margins. Section 6(5) offers some assistance, by providing that, "in relation to a particular act, a person is not a public authority by virtue only of subs.(3)(b) if the nature of the act is private"; but this still leaves much scope for uncertainty. In *R (Heather) v Leonard Cheshire Foundation* (2002), the Court of Appeal specifically recognised the possibility of "hybrids" but held that the respondents, who provided long term residential care for the disabled, were not a public authority simply by virtue of the fact that they received public funding.

In *Poplar Housing and Regeneration Community Association Ltd v Donoghue* (2002), the Court of Appeal said that the definition of who was a public authority and what was a public function, for the purposes of s.6, should be given a generous interpretation. However, the fact that a body performed an activity that otherwise a public body would be under a duty to perform, could not mean that such performance was necessarily a public function. An act could remain of a private nature even though it was performed because another body was under a public duty to ensure that that act was performed.

2–04 Section 13 is intended to offer further comfort to religious organisations in particular. It provides:

> "If a court's determination of any question arising under this Act might affect the exercise by a religious organisation (itself or its members collectively) of the Convention right to freedom of thought, conscience and religion, it must have particular regard to the importance of that right."

The Home Secretary, in the House of Commons, emphasised the requirement to have particular regard to the right to freedom of thought, conscience and religion and said that the

> "intention is to focus the courts' attention in any proceedings on the view generally held by the Church in question, and on its interest in protecting the integrity of the common faith of its members against attack, whether by outsiders or by individual dissidents" (Hansard, May 20, 1998).

This is consistent with art.17 of ECHR, which provides:

> "Nothing in this Convention may be interpreted as implying for any State, group or person any right to engage in any activity or perform any act aimed at the destruction of any of the rights and freedoms set forth herein or at their limitation to a greater extent than is provided for in the Convention."

It was the intention of those who drafted the Convention that persons of malicious intent should not be provided with a tool to subvert the rights the Convention seeks to guarantee.

"Act"

The scope of the word "act" is reasonably straightforward. In its positive **2–05** aspect, its meaning seems clear without elaboration. In addition, s.6(6) provides that "an act", for the purposes of the section, includes a failure to act. This brings us back to the concept of the positive obligation, which was discussed in Ch.1. Public authorities can take no comfort from the fact that the Convention rights are couched in negative terms. Many of them involve positive obligations and if the authority does not discharge those obligations it will find itself in difficulties. Here, we can take two (out of many potential) examples from the Convention case law. Others will arise elsewhere in the book.

The first example is *Plattform "Ärzte für das Leben" v Austria* (1991) in which the Strasbourg Court found that the art.11 right to freedom of peaceful assembly involves a positive obligation on the state to take reasonable and appropriate measures to enable lawful demonstrations to proceed peacefully. In that case, it was held to have been sufficient for the police to interpose themselves between the applicants (a pro-life organisation) who had been holding an open air religious service and those who were seeking to disrupt that service with loudspeakers and by throwing eggs. In the second example, however, the state was found to have failed in its positive obligation.

The case was *López Ostra v Spain* (1994). A plant for the treatment of tannery waste was built on municipal land 12 metres away from the applicant's home. It began to operate without the requisite licence and its start-up released fumes, smells and contamination that immediately caused health problems and nuisance to people living in the applicant's district. The local authority was substantially ineffective in dealing with the problem and the applicant and her family had to move house as a result.

The Court held that severe environmental pollution may affect individuals' well-being and prevent them from enjoying their homes in such a way as to affect their private and family life adversely even if it did not endanger their health. Although the local authority was not directly responsible for the emissions it could not be unaware that the environmental problems continued after the partial shutdown. The national authorities had not taken the positive measures necessary for protecting the applicant's right to respect for her home and for her private and family life and so there was a breach of art.8.

It would seem, then, that one effect of HRA s.6 is to impose on public authorities a duty to use such means as are within their power to promote and protect the enjoyment of the Convention rights even where the interference or threatened interference comes from a private individual or corporation. It has to be stressed that, in *López Ostra*, the Court made it clear that the duty is not absolute. A balance has to be struck between the rights of the individuals concerned. What a public authority that has the power to intervene will not be able to do, however, is simply stand back and let the individuals fight the issue out between themselves.

The effect of unlawfulness

2–06 Section 7(1) and (6) provide that a person who claims that a public authority has acted (or proposes to act) in a way which is made unlawful by s.6(1) may bring proceedings against the authority under the HRA in the appropriate court or tribunal or rely on the Convention right or rights concerned in any legal proceedings brought by or at the instigation of a public authority. In *Re S; re W* (2002), Lord Nicholls of Birkenhead said that "sections 7 and 8 are to be given a generous interpretation, as befits their human rights purpose". This is subject to the qualification that the person concerned must be, in Convention terms, a victim of the unlawful act.

The Court held in *Klass v Germany* (1979–1980) that, if they were to be successful, an individual applicant will have to be able to claim to have been actually affected by the violation they allege (In *R (on the application of Holub) v Secretary of State for the Home Department* (2001), the Court of Appeal did, however, point out that the parents of a child whose right is affected have standing as victims). The Convention does not permit individuals to complain against a law in the abstract simply because they feel that it contravenes the Convention. It is necessary that the law should have been applied to the significant disadvantage of the applicant; though the Court has held that a law may by itself violate the rights of an individual if the individual is directly affected by the law in the absence of any specific measure of implementation. An example of such a case is *Norris v Ireland* (1991) in which a homosexual man was held to be entitled to complain about legislation which rendered persons carrying out homosexual acts liable to prosecution even though he had not himself been prosecuted and in practice the law was only actually operated where a minor was involved.

Subsection (5) provides that proceedings under subs.(1)(a) must be brought before the end of the period of one year beginning with the date on which the act complained of took place or such longer period as the court or tribunal considers equitable having regard to all the circumstances (subject to any rule imposing a stricter time limit in relation to the procedure in question).

Section 8(1) HRA provides that, in relation to any act (or proposed act) **2–07** of a public authority that the court finds is (or would be) unlawful, it may grant such relief or remedy, or make such order, within its powers as it considers just and appropriate. This seems to make it clear that the HRA does not create any special procedures or new remedies. Rather, it gives new grounds for existing remedies. It also puts certain limits on courts dealing with Convention rights based issues. In particular, subs.(3) provides that:

> "No award of damages is to be made unless, taking account of all the circumstances of the case, including (a) any other relief or remedy granted, or order made, in relation to the act in question (by that or any other court), and (b) the consequences of any decision (of that or any other court) in respect of that act, the court is satisfied that the award is necessary to afford just satisfaction to the person in whose favour it is made."

As we saw in Ch.1, in many cases the Court takes the view that a simple finding of a breach is sufficient "just satisfaction". This is reinforced by subs.(4), which tells us that, in determining whether to award damages or the amount of an award the national court must take into account the principles applied by the European Court of Human Rights in relation to the award of compensation under art.41 of the Convention. Except where there is a quantifiable financial loss, the Court, if it awards compensation at all, tends to award sums which might almost be described as "token".

All of this is subject to the qualification that, in a question with a member of the ScottishGovernment, s.7(1) does not mean what it says. A question whether a purported or proposed exercise of a function by a member of the Scottish Government is, or would be incompatible with any of the Convention rights is a devolution issue for the purposes of Sch.6 to the Scotland Act 1998 and can only be pursued under the rather cumbersome devolution issue procedure set out in that Schedule and associated subordinate legislation. (In criminal cases, there is a special procedure known as the "compatibility issue" procedure.)

HUMAN RIGHTS ACT 1998 SECTION 6(2)

Introduction

2–08 Section 6(2) HRA qualifies subs.(1) by providing that it does not apply to an act if:

> "(a) as the result of one or more provisions of primary legislation, the authority could not have acted differently; or (b) in the case of one or more provisions of, or made under, primary legislation which cannot be read or given effect in a way which is compatible with the Convention rights, the authority was acting so as to give effect to or enforce those provisions."

This brings us to the whole question of the relationship between Convention rights and parliamentary sovereignty. It was the Government's clear policy, in enacting both the HRA and the Scotland Act, not to interfere with that doctrine. That policy has two manifestations that are of particular importance for this book. The first relates to the extent of, and limitations on, the requirement to interpret legislation so that it is consistent with the Convention rights; and the second relates to the limitation placed by s.6(2) on the rule that public authorities that act incompatibly with the Convention rights act unlawfully.

HUMAN RIGHTS ACT 1998 SECTIONS 2 AND 3

2–09 Section 3 HRA provides that:

> "So far as it is possible to do so, primary legislation and subordinate legislation must be read and given effect in a way which is compatible with the Convention rights."

In *R v A (Complainant's sexual history)* (2001), the House of Lords commented that the interpretative obligation under s.3 is "an emphatic adjuration by the legislature" that might sometimes necessitate the adoption of an interpretation which linguistically might appear strained. According to the House, the techniques involved will not only involve the "reading down" of express language in a statute but also the implication of provisions. For example, in *Clancy v Caird* (2000), the Inner House reasoned that, since ECHR requires security of tenure for judges to qualify as independent (for art.6 purposes), such security of tenure had to be implied.

Section 2(1) HRA provides that:

> "A court or tribunal determining a question which has arisen under the Act in connection with a Convention right must take into account any—

(a)   judgement, decision, declaration or advisory opinion of the European Court of Human Rights;
(b)   opinion of the Commission given in a report adopted under Art.31 of the Convention;
(c)   decision of the Commission in connection with Art.26 or 27(2) of the Convention; or
(d)   decision of the Committee of Ministers taken under Art.46 of the Convention,

whenever made or given, so far as, in the opinion of the court or tribunal, it is relevant to the proceedings in which that question arises."

This recognises that the use of the case law of the Court and the Commission will be essential. The obligation is, however, only to take that case law into account, not to treat it as binding. The Lord Chancellor explained at report in the House of Lords that the Convention itself has no rule of precedent and went on to say that

"should a United Kingdom court ever have a case before it which is a precise mirror of one that has been previously been considered by the European Court of Human Rights, which I doubt, it may be appropriate for it to apply the European Court's findings directly to that case; but...the courts will often be faced with cases that involve factors specific to the United Kingdom which distinguish them from cases considered by the European court" (Hansard, January 19, 1998).

In such cases, he said, and also in cases where the Strasbourg jurisprudence is out of date, it was important that UK courts should have the flexibility and discretion to develop the law.

Declarations of incompatibility

The acid test comes when a court finds it impossible to find an **2–10** interpretation of a piece of legislation which is consistent with the Convention rights. The Government's answer was clear. At Second Reading of the Human Rights Bill in the House of Lords, the Lord Chancellor said that "the Bill does not allow the courts to set aside or ignore Acts of Parliament" and that s.3 "preserves the effect of primary legislation which is incompatible with the Convention" (Hansard, November 3, 1997).

Later in the same debate, he said that the intention of the legislation was to maximise the protection to individuals "while retaining the fundamental principle of Parliamentary sovereignty". The remedy provided for the situation in which a court cannot find a way to construe legislation compatibly with the Convention rights is the declaration of incompatibility, which will not affect the validity, continuing operation or enforcement of the provision in respect of which it is given and which will not bind the parties to the proceedings in which it is made. Such a declaration might well prompt the Government to make legislative change but will not oblige it to do so. According to the House of Lords in *R v A (Complainant's sexual history)* (2001), a declaration of incompatibility is a measure of last resort that has to be avoided unless it is plainly impossible to do so.

A declaration of incompatibility can only be made, in terms of s.4(5), by superior courts—in particular:

- the Supreme Court;
- the Judicial Committee of the Privy Council;
- the Courts-Martial Appeal Court;
- the High Court of Justiciary sitting otherwise than as a trial court;
- the Court of Session;
- the High Court;
- the Court of Appeal; and
- the Court of Protection.

Stevens v Ritchie (2002) is an example of a case in which those seeking a declaration of incompatibility tried unsuccessfully to pursue the matter in the sheriff court.

3. RIGHT TO LIFE (ARTICLE 2)

INTRODUCTION

Article 2 provides: 3–01

> 1. Everyone's right to life shall be protected by law. No one shall be deprived of his life intentionally save in the execution of a sentence of a court following his conviction of a crime for which this penalty is provided by law.
>
> 2. Deprivation of life shall not be regarded as inflicted in contravention of this Article when it results from the use of force which is no more than absolutely necessary:
>
> (a)   in defence of any person from unlawful violence;
> (b)   in order to effect a lawful arrest or to prevent the escape of a person lawfully detained;
> (c)   in action lawfully taken for the purpose of quelling a riot or insurrection.

Paragraph 1 states the right:

> "Everyone's right to life shall be protected by law. No one shall be deprived of his life intentionally ... "

Paragraph 2 explains and qualifies this by setting out three sets of circumstances in which deprivation of life is not within the ambit of the article. The second part of para.1 states the permitted exception. Finally, we should note, art.2 has been held to give rise to positive obligations, which are considered below.

In *Pretty v United Kingdom* (2002) the Strasbourg Court said that art.2

> "safeguards the right to life, without which any of the other rights and freedoms in the Convention is rendered nugatory. It sets out the limited circumstances when deprivation of life may be justified and the Court has applied a strict scrutiny when those exceptions have been invoked by respondent governments ... The text of Article 2 ... has been interpreted as covering not only intentional killing but also the situations where it is permitted to use force which may result, as an unintended outcome, in the deprivation of life ... the first sentence of Article 2(1) enjoins the State not only to refrain from the intentional and unlawful taking of life but also to take appropriate steps to safeguard the lives of those within its jurisdiction ... This obligation extends beyond a primary duty to secure the right to life by putting

in place effective criminal law provisions to deter the commission of offences against the person backed up by law enforcement machinery for the prevention, suppression and sanctioning of breaches of such provisions; it may also imply in certain well defined circumstances a positive obligation to protect an individual whose life is at risk from the criminal acts of another individual".

THE SCOPE OF THE RIGHT

3–02 The most obvious application of art.2 is for deliberate killing by state officials. In fact, however, it is not so restricted. There need not be an intention to kill. In *Stewart v United Kingdom* (1984), the Commission held that art.2 was apt to cover the situation in which a soldier firing a rubber bullet at the legs of a rioter missed (because he was hit by a brick as he pulled the trigger) and the projectile struck a 12 year old boy on the head, killing him. There was no question of the boy having been killed deliberately.

Nor is it necessary for the victim to actually die before art.2 issues can arise. It is enough if their life is put at material risk. In *Yaça v Turkey* (1999), the applicant was shot by two unknown assailants. He survived and claimed that he had been shot by state officials because of his involvement in the sale of a pro-Kurdish newspaper. His uncle was shot and killed a few weeks later. The case was dealt with ultimately on the basis of the state's positive obligation to investigate but the starting point was that art.2 was applicable in the case of the applicant even though he did not die.

Because it is well recognised that the Convention is a "living instrument", to be interpreted evolutively (as described in Ch.1), it is common for those who feel that there is a gap in the law, for pressure groups and for those with concerns about particular aspects of the law to seek to use the Convention to fill the perceived gap or as a vehicle for the advancement of their chosen cause or position. This often involves arguments which seek to invest a Convention right with a rather wide meaning. Article 2 has been the subject of its share of such attention.

In *Taylor Family v United Kingdom* (1994) the Commission refused to consider the funding of the Health Service under the head of art.2 (it having been argued that financial cut backs had led to inadequate supervision which had allowed a nurse to murder babies in hospital) and in *Association X v United Kingdom* (1978) it concluded that, although a small proportion of children who had received a particular vaccination had suffered brain damage or death, overall the system for ensuring the safety of the vaccinations was a responsible one and properly administered which complied with art.2.

3–03   In general, it can be said that attempts to invoke art.2 in order to attack clinical decisions made in accordance with respectable bodies of medical opinion have not been successful (see, for example, *Re A (Children) (Conjoined Twins: Surgical Separation)* (2001) and *NHS Trust A v M* (2001)).

Questions have been raised about the effect of art.2 in relation to abortion and euthanasia. In *Vo v France* (2004), a Grand Chamber summarised the position with regard to abortion as follows:

> "Article 2 of the Convention is silent as to the temporal limitations of the right to life and, in particular, does not define 'everyone' ('toute personne') whose 'life' is protected by the Convention ... Abortion does not constitute one of the exceptions expressly listed in paragraph 2 of Article 2 but the Commission has expressed the opinion that it is compatible with the first sentence of Article 2(1) in the interests of protecting the mother's life and health because 'if one assumes that this provision applies at the initial stage of the pregnancy, the abortion is covered by an implied limitation, protecting the life and health of the woman at that stage, of the "right to life" of the foetus'."

The Court went on to say, however, that the Convention institutions had not ruled out the possibility that in certain circumstances safeguards might be extended to the unborn child. But, in *Vo*, the Court said that the issue of when the right to life begins comes within the margin of appreciation enjoyed by States, essentially because it was unable to discern any European consensus on the question. "At best", the Court said, "it may be regarded as common ground between states that the embryo/foetus belongs to the human race". The Court took the same approach in *Evans v United Kingdom* (2007), holding that UK legislation which allowed one partner to withdraw his consent to the storage and use of jointly created embryos did not breach art.2.

In relation to euthanasia, the Court said explicitly in *Pretty v United Kingdom* (2002) that a "right to die" or even a right to assisted suicide, cannot be derived from art.2 as to do so would require "distortion of language".

"Absolutely necessary"

Paragraph 2 takes a killing outside the scope of art.2 where it is in defence **3–04** of any person from unlawful violence, in order to effect a lawful arrest or to prevent the escape of a person lawfully detained or in action lawfully taken for the purpose of quelling a riot or insurrection. These exceptions have it in common that the force used must be "absolutely necessary".

In *McCann v United Kingdom* (1995), an SAS unit shot IRA members who, according to intelligence, were in Gibraltar in order to plant a bomb. The Court found against the state because, although the soldiers who shot the terrorist suspects had acted reasonably in opening fire when they thought a bomb was about to be detonated, those organising the counterterrorist operation could have avoided the possibility of such shooting by choosing to have the suspects detained at an earlier stage.

By contrast, in *Andronicou and Constantinou v Cyprus* (1997) the Court held that the use of lethal force had been absolutely necessary in a siege where a man armed with a shotgun held a hostage and the authorities tried everything they could up to the deadline set by the man before storming the flat.

Other cases on the same point include *Wolfgram v FRG* (1986), in which the Commission held that police officers had been entitled to open fire when a suspect threw a grenade at them, and *Diaz Ruano v Spain* (1994), in which (with some dissent) the Commission held that when a man being interviewed by the police seized one officer's gun and shot at the other officer the officer who had been shot at was entitled to fire back, killing the man. In *Giuliani and Gaggio v Italy* (2011) the Court held that there was no breach when a protestor was killed during a sudden and violent attack that posed an imminent and serious threat to the lives of three law enforcement officers.

Specified objectives

3–05 Granted that the force used is no more than absolutely necessary, it must still pursue one of the objectives specified in art.2.2, which the Commission said in *Stewart*, are exhaustive and must be interpreted narrowly. *McCann, Andronicou, Wolfgram* and *Diaz Ruano* are all examples of the use of force in defence against unlawful violence and the way in which the Court has handled that issue.

There have been no cases that clearly exemplify the justified use of lethal force in the course of an arrest. *Aytekin v Turkey* (1997) is an example of the unjustified use of force in such a case—the Commission considered that there was a breach of art.2 where, with the intention of stopping a car proceeding slowly through a checkpoint in such a way as to pose no risk of harm to those manning the checkpoint, a police officer shot and killed the driver.

In *Kelly v United Kingdom* (1993) the use of lethal force at a checkpoint was held to have been justified but that was in relation to a vehicle which was being driven so aggressively as to put the soldiers manning the checkpoint at risk, so as to bring the case within the defence against unlawful violence exception.

Stewart is an example of the third category. The Commission was not impressed with the argument made by the applicant that 150 people throwing missiles at a patrol of soldiers did not constitute a riot and held that an accidental death caused by the use of rubber bullets to try to quell that riot did amount to action lawfully taken for that purpose.

Capital punishment

3–06 The specific exception provided for by art.2.1 is for capital punishment. As regards the United Kingdom, this will not arise directly because the law no longer provides for the death penalty and the UK has acceded to Protocol 13 ECHR, which provides for the abolition of the death penalty in all circumstances. The point might, however, arise indirectly. It was held by the Court in *Kirkwood v United Kingdom* (1984) and *Soering v United Kingdom* (1989) that extradition to a country where the applicant might face the death penalty does not as such breach the Convention though there might be a breach of art.3 if the prison conditions likely to be applied to the applicant in the country requesting extradition are sufficiently bad.

Positive obligation

There are two aspects to the positive obligation which should take our **3–07** attention. The first of these is that in the case of a death as a result of the activities of state officials, there must be a thorough and impartial investigation, usually in public. The Strasbourg Court made that point in *McCann* and commented favourably on the inquest proceedings that had taken place. By contrast, in *Yaça* the Court held that the mere fact that the authorities had been informed of the murder of the applicant's uncle had given rise to an obligation under art.2 to carry out an effective investigation. The Turkish Government had provided no concrete information on the state of progress of the investigations which, more than five years after the events, did not appear to have produced any tangible result or have made any credible headway. In consequence there had been a violation of art.2.

Secondly, there is the question of the extent to which the police should respond to a threat to the life of an individual. This has been addressed in the case of *Osman v United Kingdom* (2000) in which a teacher, who had formed an irrational and entirely inappropriate attachment to one of his pupils, committed a number of minor offences of vandalism in furtherance of that attachment and then went on to kill the boy's father and another person. The family sought to sue the police for failing to protect them adequately and the Court said, in this context, that where the authorities know of a real and immediate threat to a person's life there is an obligation to take preventive operational measures to protect that person. The Court stressed, however, that the obligation is not to be interpreted so as to impose an impossible or disproportionate burden on the authorities. It is, for example, clear that the authorities are not required to maintain a bodyguard where the risk is a general one, such as that associated with holding public office in Ireland at the height of the troubles (*W v United Kingdom* (1983)). This may be contrasted with *Edwards v United Kingdom* (2002). In that case, the applicant's mentally ill son was arrested and remanded in custody where he was killed by his cellmate—a man who had a history of violence including assault on a previous cellmate. A subsequent inquiry found what the Court was to call a "series of shortcomings in the transmission of information". Although the police, the Crown Prosecution Services ("CPS") and the magistrates all knew that the cellmate was dangerous, no one told the prison. Nor was any information made available to the prison about his criminal or medical history. He was screened on his arrival at the prison by an inadequately trained health worker, without a doctor available for consultation. Similar shortcomings meant that Edwards' fundamental vulnerability was not recognised. The Court expressed the view that it is "self evident" that the screening process of new arrivals in a prison should serve to identify effectively those prisoners who require to be placed under medical supervision. That process failed in this case because of the defects in the provision of information and the inadequacy of the screening arrangements themselves. The Court held, therefore, that there had been a breach of art.2. In *Renolde v France* (2008), a breach was found where a man who suffered an acute psychotic illness committed suicide in prison. He had attempted suicide three days earlier. The authorities were held to have failed in their positive obligation to protect his life by (amongst other things) failing to consider whether he should have been placed in a psychiatric institution and failing to supervise his medication.

4. PROHIBITION OF TORTURE (ARTICLE 3)

INTRODUCTION

Article 3 is in uncompromising and unqualified terms: **4–01**

> "No one shall be subjected to torture or to inhuman or degrading treatment or punishment."

This identifies three species of mistreatment:
* torture;
* inhuman treatment or punishment; and
* degrading treatment or punishment.

These things are not synonymous and the Court does not treat every unwarranted application of violence as a breach of art.3. In the *Greek Interstate Case* (1969) the Commission distinguished acts prohibited by art.3 from what it called a "certain roughness of treatment" which might take the form of slaps or blows of the hand on the face or the head. The Commission considered that, although such treatment is to be condemned on moral grounds (and might in some circumstances amount to a breach of art.8) it did not amount to a breach of art.3. However, the Court did make it clear, in *Ribitsch v Austria* (1996) that, in respect of a person deprived of their liberty, any use of physical force which has not been made strictly necessary by their own conduct diminishes human dignity and is in principle an infringement of the right set forth in art.3 of the Convention. The requirements of an investigation and the undeniable difficulties inherent in the fight against crime could not, the Court said, justify placing limits on the protection to be afforded in respect of the physical integrity of individuals. The reference to "force not made necessary by the person's own conduct" is illustrated by *Caloc v France* (2002) in which the applicant complained that, whilst in custody in connection with vandalism, he had been thrown to the ground and beaten. His injuries were minor. He admitted that he had attempted to escape and that in so doing he had put up resistance to the police and jostled them. In these circumstances, the Court was not sympathetic to his application.

TORTURE

Torture was defined in *Ireland v United Kingdom* (1979–1980) as **4–02**
"deliberate inhuman treatment causing *very serious and cruel suffering*" [emphasis added].

A very clear example of the kind of conduct which will amount to torture is to be found in *Aydin v Turkey* (1998). In that case, the applicant was a 17 year old Turkish citizen of Kurdish origin. She was detained and taken to the local police headquarters. There she was blindfolded, beaten, stripped, placed inside a tyre and sprayed with high pressure water, and raped. It appeared probable that the applicant was subjected to such treatment because it was suspected that she or other members of her family had collaborated with Kurdish separatists.

The Court said that, in order to determine whether any particular form of ill treatment should be qualified as torture, regard must be had to the distinction drawn in art.3 between this notion and that of inhuman treatment or degrading treatment. This distinction had been embodied in the Convention to allow the special stigma of "torture" to attach only to deliberate inhuman treatment causing very serious and cruel suffering. The Court was satisfied that the accumulation of acts of physical and mental violence inflicted on the applicant and the especially cruel act of rape to which she was subjected amounted to torture in breach of art.3.

The threshold for what will constitute very serious and cruel suffering is not fixed. In *Selmouni v France* (2000), the applicant had been arrested and questioned over several days in connection with alleged drug trafficking. Subsequent medical examination found that he presented "lesions of traumatic origin on his skin that were sustained at a time which corresponds to the period of police custody". Police officers were subsequently convicted of assaulting him. The Court reiterated that it must have regard to the distinction between the concept of torture and that of inhuman or degrading treatment. It was clear that the treatment to which Selmouni had been subjected was sufficiently serious to be characterised as inhuman and degrading but not that it was serious enough to amount to torture. The Court recalled that the Convention is a "living instrument which must be interpreted in the light of present-day conditions". It said that certain acts which were classified in the past as "inhuman and degrading treatment" as opposed to "torture" could be classified differently in future. It took the view that the increasingly high standard being required in the area of the protection of human rights and fundamental liberties correspondingly and inevitably requires greater firmness in assessing breaches of the fundamental values of democratic societies. It found that the conduct to which Selmouni had been subjected amounted to torture.

In determining whether conduct amounts to torture, the Court lays some emphasis on the purpose for which violence is used. If that purpose is to obtain information or a confession from a person suspected of involvement in crime, the Court is more likely to regard the conduct as amounting to torture. That motive was significant in *Ireland v United Kingdom* (1979–1980) and also in *Dikme v Turkey* (2000). In *Dikme*, a suspect was interrogated with considerable brutality and electrodes were applied to his feet, ears and genitals. The Court considered that this treatment had been inflicted on him intentionally by servants of the state in the performance of their duties with the aim of extracting from him confessions or information about offences. That being so, taking all these acts of violence against the applicant's person together, and having regard to the length of time for which they had lasted and their purpose, the Court considered they had been particularly serious and cruel, so that they must have caused Dikme "acute" pain and suffering. They accordingly warranted the classification of torture within the meaning of art.3.

INHUMAN TREATMENT

In *Ireland v United Kingdom*, the treatment complained of included keeping **4–03** detainees' heads covered by a hood, subjecting them to continuous loud noise, depriving them of sleep, depriving them of food and making them stand against a wall for hours at a time with their feet widely separated. This, it was held, was inhuman treatment but did not occasion suffering of the particular intensity and cruelty implied by the word "torture".

DEGRADING TREATMENT

In *Tyrer v United Kingdom* (1979–1980), the Court explained that, for a **4–04** punishment to be "degrading" and in breach of art.3, the humiliation or debasement involved must attain a particular level and must in any event be other than the usual element of humiliation involved in judicial punishment. The assessment is relative and depends on all the circumstances and, in particular, on the nature and context of the punishment itself and the manner and method of its execution. That case established that judicial corporal punishment (i.e. that inflicted by the state) is likely to constitute degrading treatment. Other examples of degrading treatment include:

- *Iwanczuk v Poland* (2004), in which the applicant, upon requesting permission to vote in a local election whilst detained on remand, had been ordered to undress in front of a group of guards who searched him and then taunted him about his physique.
- *Dougoz v Greece* (2002), in which the applicant was held for several months in police stations where cells were seriously overcrowded. The sanitary facilities were appalling, hot water was scarce, there was no fresh air or natural light and there was no yard in which to exercise.
- *Gutsanovi v Bulgaria* (2013), in which a prominent local politician with no history of violence was arrested at home in the early hours of the morning by a team of armed and masked police officers. No consideration had been given to the presence of the applicant's wife and two young children or to the psychological effect on them.
- *Price v United Kingdom* (2002). The applicant was four-limb deficient as a result of thalidomide. She also suffered from problems with her kidneys. She was imprisoned by a civil court for refusing to answer questions put to her concerning her financial position in a debt recovery action against her, without any enquiry being made

about the availability of suitable conditions in which to keep her. The Strasbourg Court noted that the assessment of the level of severity of treatment is relative and depends on all the circumstances of the case, including, in some cases, the sex, age and state of health of the victim. While there was no evidence of any positive intention to humiliate or debase the applicant, the Court considered that to detain a severely disabled person in conditions where she was dangerously cold, risked developing sores because her bed is too hard or unreachable, and was unable to go to the toilet without the assistance of male prison officers or keep clean without the greatest of difficulty, constituted degrading treatment.

- *Mouisel v France* (2004), in which a prisoner was chained unnecessarily whilst undergoing chemotherapy for leukaemia. See also *Kashavelov v Bulgaria* (2011), in which the Court found that the routine handcuffing of a prisoner whenever he was outside his cell was degrading.

With these, one may contrast *Kudla v Poland* (2002), in which a prisoner on remand attempted suicide twice. There was no evidence to demonstrate that his suicide attempts had been prompted by any shortcomings on the part of the authorities, hence, no breach was found. In *R v Governor of HMP Frankland Ex p. Russell* (2000), it was held (following *McFeeley v United Kingdom* (1980)) that it is not degrading to require prison inmates to wear prison clothes (but that it might well be degrading or worse to sanction refusal by cutting their meals to one a day). Moreover, solitary confinement does not, in itself, amount to degrading or inhuman behaviour and is permissible in order to protect a prisoner from other prisoners (*Re Fulton's Application for Judicial Review* (2001)).

BURDEN OF PROOF

4–05 The Court held in *Ribitsch* and again in *Selmouni* that where an individual is taken into police custody in good health but is found to be injured at the time of release, it is incumbent on the state to provide a plausible explanation of how those injuries were caused, failing which a clear issue arises under art.3 of the Convention. Absent an innocent explanation for Selmouni's injuries, the state had prima facie failed to meet its obligation under art.3 of the Convention to ensure that he was not subjected to torture or to inhuman or degrading treatment.

ARTICLE 3 AND EXTRADITION OR DEPORTATION

4–06 There is, as the Court said in *Soering v United Kingdom* (1989), no right in ECHR not to be extradited. Indeed, there is only one reference to extradition in ECHR (art.5.1(f)) and that reference does not create a right.

On the contrary, it qualifies the art.5 right to liberty and security of person by specifying detention with a view to extradition as one of the permitted exceptions to the rule that persons are not to be deprived of their liberty. But, as the Court went on to say in *Soering*

> "in so far as a measure of extradition has consequences adversely affecting the enjoyment of a Convention right it may, assuming the consequences are not too remote, attract the obligations of a Contracting State under the relevant Convention guarantee".

In particular, in *Soering* and certain other cases, the Court has held that it would be a breach of art.3 to extradite or deport someone to a jurisdiction where they are likely to be subject to treatment which, if it occurred in the respondent state, would breach that article. In *Soering*, the Court said that art.3 enshrines one of the fundamental values of the democratic societies making up the Council of Europe and that it would not be compatible with the underlying values of the Convention if a contracting state were knowingly to surrender a fugitive to another state where there were substantial grounds for believing that they would be in danger of being subjected to torture, however heinous the crime allegedly committed. In the Court's view, this inherent obligation not to extradite also extended to cases in which the fugitive would be faced in the receiving State by a real risk of exposure to inhuman or degrading treatment or punishment proscribed by art.3. The Secretary of State's decision to extradite the applicant to Virginia would, if implemented, give rise to a breach of art.3 because the applicant might there be subject to the "death row phenomenon", spending many years in a condemned cell awaiting execution.

Jabari v Turkey (2000) is another example. The applicant was an Iranian woman who had fallen in love with a man whose family was opposed to their marriage. He married another woman but they continued to see each other and to have sexual intercourse. They were discovered and arrested for adultery, the penalty for which in Iran was death by stoning or flogging. Understandably enough, when the applicant was fortunate enough to be set at liberty through the intervention of relatives, she fled the country and entered Turkey on a false passport. She was arrested and ordered to be deported. She applied to the Court, which found it substantiated that there was a real risk of the applicant being subjected to treatment contrary to art.3 if returned to Iran and accordingly her deportation, if carried out, would give rise to a violation of art.3.

Positive obligation

Article 3 carries with it a positive obligation to provide protection through **4–07** the legal system against a person suffering, at the hands of others, treatment which breaches the art.3 standards. One aspect of that obligation is the provision of a means of bringing to justice those who commit serious acts of violence against others. So, in *MC v Bulgaria* (2003), the Strasbourg

Human Rights

Court found that there was a breach of art.3 because Bulgarian law still dealt with rape in a way which required physical force. Also on the basis of the positive obligation, in *R (B) v Director of Public Prosecutions* (2009), the Divisional Court found a breach of art.3 where a prosecution for serious assault was discontinued by the Crown Prosecution Service on inadequate grounds.

5. RIGHT TO LIBERTY (ARTICLE 5)

INTRODUCTION

Article 5 provides: 5–01

1. Everyone has the right to liberty and security of person. No one shall be deprived of his liberty save in the following cases and in accordance with a procedure prescribed by law:

a. the lawful detention of a person after conviction by a competent court;

b. the lawful arrest or detention of a person for non- compliance with the lawful order of a court or in order to secure the fulfilment of any obligation prescribed by law;

c. the lawful arrest or detention of a person effected for the purpose of bringing him before the competent legal authority on reasonable suspicion of having committed an offence or when it is reasonably considered necessary to prevent his committing an offence or fleeing after having done so;

d. the detention of a minor by lawful order for the purpose of educational supervision or his lawful detention for the purpose of bringing him before the competent legal authority;

e. the lawful detention of persons for the prevention of the spreading of infectious diseases, of persons of unsound mind, alcoholics or drug addicts or vagrants;

f. the lawful arrest or detention of a person to prevent his effecting an unauthorised entry into the country or of a person against whom action is being taken with a view to deportation or extradition.

2. Everyone who is arrested shall be informed promptly, in a language which he understands, of the reasons for his arrest and of any charge against him.

3. Everyone arrested or detained in accordance with the provisions of para.1.c of this article shall be brought promptly before a judge or other officer authorised by law to exercise judicial power and shall be entitled to trial within a reasonable time or to release pending trial. Release may be conditioned by guarantees to appear for trial.

4. Everyone who is deprived of his liberty by arrest or detention shall be entitled to take proceedings by which the lawfulness of his detention shall be decided speedily by a court and his release ordered if the detention is not lawful.

5. Everyone who has been the victim of arrest or detention in contravention of the provisions of this article shall have an enforceable right to compensation.

As can be seen, art.5.1 begins by stating the general right: "Everyone has the right to liberty and security of person". It then states the permitted exceptions to the right:

"No one shall be deprived of his liberty save in the following cases and in accordance with a procedure prescribed by law."

Six subparagraphs then set out the cases in which deprivation of liberty is permitted. They are exhaustive and fall to be construed narrowly (*Monnell and Morris v United Kingdom* (1987)). If a deprivation of liberty cannot be brought within one of these six cases, it necessarily involves a breach of art.5.1 (*Ciulla v Italy* (1991)). Given a deprivation of liberty for the purposes of art.5, the authority responsible for that deprivation must, if it is to avoid a finding of breach, bring the case within one of the permitted exceptions to the right. It should be noted, however, that the mere fact that the decision to deprive a person of their liberty is overturned on appeal will not by itself establish a breach of art.5.1 (*Perks v United Kingdom* (1999)).

DEPRIVATION OF LIBERTY

5–02 The first question in relation to art.5 will always be whether there has been a deprivation of liberty. The answer will depend on the particular facts of the case under consideration. It should be noted that the concept of deprivation of liberty has been contrasted with the more limited idea of restrictions on freedom of movement. In *Engel v the Netherlands* (1979–1980), the confining of military personnel to barracks did not amount to a deprivation of liberty but locking them up did. It is not, however, necessary that the person concerned should have been arrested or detained formally for there to be a deprivation of liberty. The concept includes any element of compulsion restricting a person to a particular location. So the confinement of asylum seekers "air-side" at an airport (*Amuur v France* (1996)) and the confinement to an hotel of sect members undergoing deprogramming (*Riera-Blume v Spain* (1999)) have both constituted deprivation of liberty for the purposes of art.5. Nevertheless, the placing in a nursing home of a pensioner who, as a result of neglect and dementia, was not coping living in a house belonging to her son was held not to be a deprivation of liberty but, rather, a responsible measure taken in the applicant's own interests in order to provide her with the necessary medical care and adequate living conditions (*HM v Switzerland* (2004)). In *S v Airedale National Health Service Trust* (2002) it was held that a patient already lawfully detained under the Mental Health Act who was placed under seclusion was not deprived of his liberty because the seclusion affected the conditions of existing detention rather than constituting detention as such.

PROCEDURE PRESCRIBED BY LAW

The Court has said in cases such as *Winterwerp v the Netherlands* (1980) **5–03** and *Steel v United Kingdom* (1999) that there must be full compliance with domestic law and also that the applicable domestic law be formulated with sufficient precision to allow the citizen—if need be with legal advice—to foresee to a reasonable degree the legal consequences of any given action. It has been held in other contexts under the Convention that common law rules are, in principle, adequate to satisfy this requirement (for example, *Sunday Times v United Kingdom* (1980) and *CR v United Kingdom; SW v United Kingdom* (1995)).

It is important to recognise that lawfulness in domestic law is not by itself decisive. In *Erkalo v the Netherlands* (1997) the application by the authorities to extend the period during which the applicant was detained compulsorily in a mental hospital was misfiled by the court and not dealt with until well after the authority to so detain him had expired. Although the national court agreed with the applicant's submission that the application was out of time and therefore in principle no longer admissible, it nonetheless declined to order his release, considering that it was imperative to the public interest that he remain in detention. No appeal lay against this decision.

The Court held that the lawfulness of the extension of the applicant's placement under domestic law is not in itself decisive. It must also be established that his detention during the period under consideration was in conformity with the purpose of art.5.1 of the Convention, namely to protect individuals from arbitrariness. Although all the relevant authorities had been aware that the applicant's placement was due to expire, none of them took any steps to verify whether the request had been received at the registry of the national court and whether a date had been fixed for a hearing on the request. The detention of the applicant after expiry of the original order was not compatible with the purpose of art.5 and was for that reason unlawful.

THE SIX CASES

Conviction

The first case in which deprivation of liberty is permitted under the **5–04** Convention is, in terms of art.5.1(a) the lawful detention of a person after conviction by a competent court. This, of course, deals with a sentence of imprisonment and, although it is straightforward for the most part, there have been questions about what constitutes a "court" for the purposes of subpara.(a) and what connection there has to be between the conviction and the detention to satisfy the subparagraph.

The word "court" was considered in *De Wilde, Ooms and Versyp v Belgium* (1979–1980), in which the Court said that the word "court" implies common elements where it is used in arts 2.1, 5.1(a) and (b), 5.4 and 6.1. Those elements are:

- independence of the executive and of the parties to the case; and
- the guarantees of judicial procedure.

In *De Wilde*, the procedure in question was that of the detention of vagrants where the Belgian authorities explain that the Code of Criminal Procedure did not apply, even though the consequence of the proceedings was detention which lasted, in the case of one of the applicants, for 21 months. The Court held, therefore, that the police court in which the detention was ordered did not satisfy the Convention definition of a "court".

The question of the connection between the conviction and the detention was considered in *Weeks v United Kingdom* (1987). The applicant had been sentenced to life imprisonment for armed robbery. He was released on licence three times but each time his licence was revoked. He argued that his detention following revocation did not amount to lawful detention after conviction by a competent court. The Court, however, noted that the possibility of revocation was inherent in the concept of the life sentence and that each revocation had been triggered by conduct on the part of the applicant which had given cause for concern (especially where he had been assessed, in connection with the imposition of the sentence, as dangerous). The Court therefore found sufficient connection between the sentence and the revocations. The House of Lords reached the same conclusion in *R v Parole Board (Smith)* (2005).

Court orders and obligations prescribed by law
5–05 Article 5.1(b) permits the arrest or detention of a person in two situations:
- for non-compliance with the lawful order of a court; and
- to secure the fulfilment of any obligation prescribed by law.

The first part of this is concerned with the sort of thing that could lead to a finding of contempt of court. It has, for example, been held to apply to failure to make a declaration of assets ordered by a court (*X v FRG* (1983)). It does not, however, permit imprisonment for failure to comply with a contractual obligation (for example, failure to pay a debt even after litigation in which the creditor has been successful). Such imprisonment is specifically excluded by the Fourth Protocol to ECHR and although the UK is not a party to that protocol the commentators agree that this does not mean that imprisonment for debt is permitted in the UK by art.5.1(b).

Imprisonment in respect of failure to pay a fine, on the other hand, is permitted (*Airey v Ireland* (1977)).

One might have thought it self-evident that there can be no question of non-compliance with a court order if the person concerned has not been told about the existence of the order. However, in *Petukhova v Russia*

(2013) the Court found it necessary to reaffirm previous case law which decided that what is required is that the person should be told of the order and given an opportunity to comply. In that case, the applicant (who was alleged to have been behaving in a bizarre way) was detained in a police station for four hours for a court ordered psychiatric examination about which she had not been told.

In *Engel v the Netherlands* (1979–1980), the Court explained that the second leg, permitting detention to secure the fulfilment of any obligation prescribed by law, concerns cases

> "where the law permits the detention of a person to compel him to fulfil a specific and concrete obligation which he has until then failed to satisfy"

but not internment meant to compel a citizen to discharge his general duty of obedience to the law. Examples of obligations which are relevant to art.5.1(b) have included an obligation to make customs or tax returns (*McVeigh, O'Neill and Evans v United Kingdom* (1981)).

Suspicion of crime
Article 5.1(c) permits 5–06

> "the lawful arrest or detention of a person effected for the purpose of bringing him before the competent legal authority on reasonable suspicion of having committed an offence or when it is reasonably considered necessary to prevent his committing an offence or fleeing having done so".

The preventative arrest which this contemplates and the possibility of arrest to prevent flight have hardly been addressed by the Strasbourg authorities (though in *Lukanov v Bulgaria* (1997) the Commission held that the state's right to arrest to prevent flight depends on the existence of reasonable suspicion that the person concerned has in fact committed an offence). Deprivation of liberty to prevent flight following the commission of an offence is, however, very common.

Taken literally, the requirement that deprivation of liberty should have the purpose of placing the person detained before the court would mean that deprivation of liberty would breach the Convention unless that person was both kept in custody and presented to the court. In other words, the police and the prosecutor could not safely decide to liberate the accused having once arrested them. In *Brogan v United Kingdom* (1989), however, the Court declined to take that approach. It said that art.5.1(c) does not presuppose that the police should have obtained sufficient evidence to bring charges and proceeded on the basis that it is legitimate to detain so as to further an investigation and that, if sufficient evidence was obtained during that investigation, no doubt the person detained would be put before the court.

In *Brogan* the persons detained were not in fact placed before the court (because there was insufficient evidence after investigation). The Court did not find a breach of the Convention in that regard.

Reasonable suspicion refers to the existence of facts or information that would satisfy an independent observer that the person concerned might have committed the offence (*Fox, Campbell and Hartley v United Kingdom* (1990)) but full proof is not necessary (*X v Austria* (1989)) (otherwise *Brogan* could not have been decided as it was).

Detention of minors

5–07   Article 5.1(d) permits the detention of a minor for two purposes:
- educational supervision; or
- in order to bring him before the competent legal authority.

Neither of these has been very fully considered by the Commission or the Court. So far as educational supervision goes, the clearest case is *Bouamar v Belgium* (1987), which establishes only that to detain a 16-year-old in a remand prison without any educational facilities for a total of 119 days in a year is not justified by art.5.1(d). The only surprise in that is that the Belgian Government thought it worth arguing that the subparagraph did justify the remand. On the other hand, in *Koniarska v United Kingdom* (2000), the Court found that the detention of an applicant aged 17 under a secure accommodation order was justified under this provision. The Court considered that, in the context of the detention of minors, "educational supervision" should not be equated rigidly with notions of classroom teaching. It should, particularly in a care context, embrace many aspects of the exercise by the local authority of parental rights for the benefits and protection of the child concerned.

The second leg, which permits detention in order to bring a minor before the competent legal authority, is generally understood as equivalent to art.5.1(c), though it does not state the elements relating to reasonable suspicion of having committed a criminal offence.

Mental illness and vagrancy

5–08   Article 5.1(e) permits the detention of five groups of persons:
- those whom it is necessary to detain in order to prevent the spread of infectious diseases;
- persons of unsound mind;
- alcoholics;
- drug addicts; and
- vagrants.

The only cases to have gone before the Court have related to persons of unsound mind and to vagrants.

In *Winterwerp v Netherlands* (1979–1980) the Court held that the term "persons of unsound mind" cannot be given a definitive interpretation. It said, however, that the term cannot refer simply to someone whose views or behaviour deviate from the norms prevailing in a particular society because that would not be reconcilable with art.5.1, whose object and purpose is to ensure that no one is dispossessed of their liberty in an arbitrary fashion and which sets out an exhaustive list of exceptions calling for a narrow interpretation. The Court approved the practice of the Netherlands courts whereby the confinement of a "mentally ill person" was authorised only if their mental disorder was of such a kind or such a gravity as to make them an actual danger to themselves or others. In *Ashingdane v United Kingdom* (1985), the Court explained that one can derive from its case law three minimum conditions that have to be satisfied in order for there to be "the lawful detention of a person of unsound mind" within the meaning of art.5.1(e):

- except in emergency cases, a true mental disorder must be established before a competent authority on the basis of objective medical expertise;
- the mental disorder must be of a kind or degree warranting compulsory confinement; and
- the validity of continued confinement depends upon the persistence of such a disorder.

In *Winterwerp*, the Court was prepared to accept that an emergency admission to hospital might extend for six weeks whilst the condition of the person concerned was being assessed, though there are indications in the judgment that the Court thought that six weeks was about the limit for that process. Also in *Ashingdane*, the Court said that held that the detention of persons of unsound mind must be in a suitable institution such as a hospital or clinic. In *Anderson v Scottish Ministers and the Advocate General* (2001), the Privy Council considered that it could not be right that public peace and safety should be subordinated to the liberty of persons whose mental states rendered them dangerous to society. It was noted that art.5(1)(e) does not require that the detention of persons of unsound mind be for the purpose of treatment, however, it should be in a hospital, clinic or other appropriate institution authorised for the purpose. Detention under art.5(1)(e) is justified where it is necessary to serve a legitimate social purpose, which may be, for example, the protection of the public.

The meaning of the term "vagrant" was considered in two cases. In *Guzzardi v Italy* (1980) it was held that it is not wide enough to include mafia suspects without identifiable sources of income; but in *De Wilde* it was held that persons with no fixed abode, no means of subsistence and no regular trade or profession were within the concept of vagrant.

Immigration and extradition

Article 5.1(f) deals with the need for detention in connection with **5–09** immigration and extradition. As the Court recognised in *Chahal v United Kingdom* (1996), states have the right, as a matter of well-established international law and subject to their treaty obligations including the Convention, to control the entry, residence and expulsion of aliens. The

Court also noted in that case that the right to political asylum is not contained in either the Convention or its Protocols.

Article 5.1(f) authorises lawful arrest or detention for three purposes:
- to prevent unlawful entry to the country;
- deportation; and
- extradition.

The lawfulness criterion proved to be particularly important in *Bozano v France* (1986). In that case, the applicant had been the subject of an extradition request to France from Italy following his conviction in absence in the Italian courts of abduction, attempted extortion, murder and various offences of indecency. The French court refused extradition on the ground that trial in absence for serious offences without any requirement to hold a retrial in the presence of the accused was incompatible with French public policy. He was released from French custody. About a month later, in Limoges, where he lived, three plain clothes policemen forced him into an unmarked car. He was taken to police headquarters and served with a deportation order that required him to leave France. He was told that it was out of the question that he should be brought before the appeals board charged with dealing with such cases and was instead placed in a car and taken, not to the Spanish border (which was the closest) but to the Swiss border, 12 hours and several hundred kilometres away. From Switzerland he was extradited to Italy and there incarcerated to serve the life sentence that had been imposed on him in his absence. It is perhaps not surprising that the Court held that, viewing the circumstances as a whole, the applicant's deprivation of liberty was neither lawful nor compatible with the right to security of person. Another example of illegality is to be found in *Conka v Belgium* (2002), in which Slovakian nationals of Romany origin had applied unsuccessfully for political asylum in Belgium. They were ordered to leave the country or be deported. The police sent a notice to them requiring them to attend the police station "to enable the files concerning their applications for asylum to be completed". When they attended, they were taken to a closed transit centre and thence to a military airport where they were put on a plane to Slovakia. This was notwithstanding the fact that their lawyer was still pursuing the appeal process and that their appeal could not have been heard before deportation took place.

MINIMUM RIGHTS FOR DETAINED PERSONS

5–10 Article 5.1 is concerned with the legitimacy of depriving a person of their liberty. The remainder of art.5 provides for certain minimum rights for a person who is in that position.

Information about the reason for detention

Article 5.2 requires that such a person should be informed "promptly" **5–11** (which means as soon as possible unless the person is in such a condition that they cannot understand what they are being told—*Clinton v United Kingdom* (1995)) in a language which they understand (fluency is not necessary) of the reasons for their arrest and of any charge against them. In *Fox, Campbell and Hartley* (1990) it was held that the art.5.2 guarantee means that the detained person must be told in simple, non-technical language that they can understand the essential legal and factual grounds for their arrest so as to be able, if they see fit, to challenge its lawfulness under art.5.4. This formula suggests that a high degree of legal precision is not required; and, indeed, it has been held in that case and others that if the process of questioning itself makes the charge clear, art.5.2 will be satisfied. Perhaps the most extreme example was *Dikme v Turkey* (2000). In that case, the Court held that when a police officer said to a suspect:

> "You belong to Devrimci Sol [a left wing terrorist group] and if you don't give us the information we need the only way for you to get out of here will be as a corpse!"

these words were sufficient to satisfy the requirements of art.5.2. The Court considered that this most reprehensible statement gave a fairly precise indication of the nature of the suspicions entertained about the applicant. Having regard to that, to the fact that the organisation mentioned was illegal and to the reasons that might have prompted the applicant to hide his identity and to fear the police, the Court considered that the applicant should or could have realised at that stage that he was suspected of being involved in prohibited activities such as those of Devrimci Sol, so that there had been no violation of art.5.2.

Trial within a reasonable time or release pending trial

Article 5(3) entitles the accused to trial within a reasonable time or to **5–12** release pending trial. It is clear that, in Convention terms, if the accused is to be kept in custody there must be relevant and sufficient grounds for doing so; but in *Tomasi v France* (1993) it was held that suspicion alone was not enough to justify a remand in custody which lasted over five years. No exhaustive list of other reasons justifying the remand of the accused in custody exists. The principle was stated by the Court in *Letellier v France* (1992) to be that the court before which the accused is brought must consider "all the facts arguing for and against the existence of a genuine requirement of public interest" for the remanding of the accused in custody. In *CC v United Kingdom* (1999) the Commission said that

> "the judge must examine all the facts arguing for and against the existence of a genuine requirement of public interest justifying, with due regard to the presumption of innocence, a departure from the rule of respect for the accused's liberty".

It is possible to classify the Strasbourg cases in four categories:
- prevention of crime;
- danger of flight;
- risk of interference with the course of justice; and
- prevention of public disorder.

This categorisation is, of course, no more than an analytical tool. As to the prevention of crime, it was held in *Toth v Austria* (1992) that previous convictions could be relied on as giving reasonable grounds to fear that further offences would be committed. The danger of flight will vary according to the strength of the accused's ties with the jurisdiction and the court should consider financial guarantees (which include, but are not limited to, money bail) as a means of offsetting the risk (*Letellier; Matznetter v Austria* (1979–1980). The risk of interference with the course of justice requires to be kept under review and, if it disappears, liberation should follow unless there are other grounds for keeping the accused in custody (*Kemmache (No.1) v France* (1992)) Finally, the cases on prevention of public disorder have related to terrorist offences (*Tomasi* (1993)) or the exceptional circumstances of a high profile, premeditated murder (*Letellier* (1992)).

Judicial determination of the lawfulness of detention
5–13 Article 5.4 provides that a person who has been deprived of their liberty must be able to take proceedings whereby the lawfulness of their detention is decided speedily by a court. This is a different issue from the appropriateness of a remand in custody, which is dealt with under art.5.3. Under art.5.4 it is the lawfulness of the detention that is in issue. In *Lamy v Belgium* (1989) it was held that the principle of equality of arms applies to art.5.4 so that the accused must be afforded the opportunity to present their case under conditions that do not place them at a substantial disadvantage vis-à-vis the prosecution.

COMPENSATION

5–14 Finally, art.5.5 requires that everyone who has been the victim of arrest or detention in contravention of art.5 shall have an enforceable right to compensation in the national courts. This is not the same as the power of the Court to award just satisfaction (*Brogan* (1989); *Fox, Campbell and Hartley* (1990)).

It is important to understand that the right to compensation does not necessarily follow from a decision taken by an appeal court that a person should be released. It has to be established that the detention was not merely inappropriate but that it was in breach of art.5. In *Perks v United Kingdom* (1999), each applicant had failed to pay sums due in respect of community charge (a politically controversial predecessor of council tax, known colloquially as "poll tax"). At the time, the applicants were dependent on state benefits or living on a low income. In separate proceedings in magistrates' courts it was established that the non-payment was due to the debtor's wilful refusal or culpable neglect. Each of the applicants were thereupon committed to a term of imprisonment and detained. Legal aid was not available and the applicants were not legally represented before the magistrates' courts. The applicants were released on bail after applying for judicial review before the High Court. Following judicial review proceedings, each applicant obtained an order quashing the magistrates' imprisonment order in their case. The Court attached importance to the reasoning of the High Court judgments in the applicants' cases. In all of them, a key ground for the decision to quash was that the magistrates had not considered the alternative ways in which to exercise the discretion vested in them. In particular, they had failed to consider alternatives to imprisonment. But the High Court left open the possibility that the imprisonment orders were within the magistrates' jurisdiction, their defect being only a fettered exercise of discretion. It could not therefore be excluded that these orders were "flawed" or "unlawful" in the sense of being an unreasonable exercise of discretion but nevertheless fell within the jurisdiction of the courts by which they were made. The Court, therefore, did not find it established that the imprisonment orders were invalid and, thus, unlawful.

6. RIGHT TO A FAIR HEARING (ARTICLE 6)

6–01 Article 6 is in these terms:

1. In the determination of his civil rights and obligations or of any criminal charge against him, everyone is entitled to a fair and public hearing within a reasonable time by an independent and impartial tribunal established by law. Judgment shall be pronounced publicly but the press and public may be excluded from all or part of the trial in the interests of morals, public order or national security in a democratic society, where the interests of juveniles or the protection of the private life of the parties so require, or to the extent strictly necessary in the opinion of the court in special circumstances where publicity would prejudice the interests of justice.

2. Everyone charged with a criminal offence shall be presumed innocent until proved guilty according to law.

3. Everyone charged with a criminal offence has the following minimum rights:

a. to be informed promptly, in a language which he understands and in detail, of the nature and cause of the accusation against him;
b. to have adequate time and facilities for the preparation of his defence;
c. to defend himself in person or through legal assistance of his own choosing or, if he has not sufficient means to pay for legal assistance, to be given it free when the interests of justice so require;
d. to examine or have examined witnesses against him and to obtain the attendance and examination of witnesses on his behalf under the same conditions as witnesses against him;
e. to have the free assistance of an interpreter if he cannot understand or speak the language used in court.

Article 6 has accounted for far more of the case law of the Strasbourg Court than any other single article. Much of it relates to criminal law.

In *Brown v Stott* (2001), Lord Hope of Craighead explained that

"the jurisprudence of the European Court tells us that the questions that should be addressed when issues are raised about an alleged incompatibility with a right under Article 6 of the Convention are the following: (1) is the right which is in question an absolute right, or is it a right which is open to modification or restriction because it is not absolute? (2) if it is not absolute, does the modification or restriction which is contended for have a legitimate aim in the public interest? (3) if so, is there a reasonable relationship of proportionality between the means employed and the aim sought to be realised? The answer to the question whether the right is or is not absolute is to be found by examining the terms of the Article in the light of the judgments of the Court. The question whether a legitimate aim is being pursued enables account to be taken of the public interest in the rule of law. The principle of proportionality directs attention to the question whether a fair balance has been struck between the general interest of the community in the realisation of that aim and the protection of the fundamental rights of the individual."

THE APPLICATION OF ARTICLE 6

It should be noted, first, that art.6 applies to the determination of civil rights **6–02** and obligations and of criminal charges. Several cases concerning civil rights and obligations have emphasised that art.6 does not apply to proceedings which do not determine civil rights or criminal charges (for example, *Brady v United Kingdom* (1980) and *Koek v Germany* (1987)). There have been fewer cases on the point arising out of criminal matters but it appears that art.6 does not apply to those parts of proceedings that do not bear upon the determination of the charge. In particular, it does not apply to proceedings relating to deprivation of liberty which do not bear on the ultimate determination of the charge because they are dealt with by art.5. In *X v Federal Republic of Germany* (1974) the applicant was a man charged with murder who complained that he had not been permitted to attend appeal proceedings relating to his remand in custody. The Commission held that, since the question of the determination of the charge did not arise, art.6 did not apply.

The Court pointed out in *Weeks v United Kingdom* (1988) that matters of sentencing in general lie outside the scope of the Convention, but did hold in *T v United Kingdom* (2000) that art.6 applies to the sentencing phase and that that phase is not complete until the sentence has been definitively set. This means that, inter alia, the sentence must be fixed by an "independent and impartial tribunal established by law". That expression was held not to describe a Home Secretary.

In *Mamatkulov and Askarov v Turkey* (2005) a Grand Chamber reiterated that art.6 does not apply to extradition proceedings.

The overriding fairness requirement

Article 6.1 contains an overriding requirement that the hearing should be **6–03** "fair" and a number of specific requirements. Compliance with the specific rights set out in art.6 will not alone guarantee that there has been a fair trial.

The Court always looks at this question in the context of the trial as a whole. The concept of the "trial as a whole" includes any appeal proceedings (*Edwards v United Kingdom* (1992); *Crociani, Palmiotti, Tanassi and Lefebre D'Ovidio v Italy* (1981)) and even where there has been unfairness in the trial itself, the Court has been prepared to hold that such unfairness has been cured by what has happened on appeal (*Edwards*). The focus of the Court may therefore be said to be on the overall process of determination of the criminal charge rather than on the set piece hearing itself.

By the same token, the focus is on the process. The case law of the Court does not comment on what the outcome of the trial should have been and even where it finds that there has been unfairness in the trial proceedings it refrains, sometimes explicitly, from saying that the accused should have been acquitted (*Saunders* (1996)). From this emphasis on fair process is derived the principle of equality of arms, by which a party is entitled to present their case under conditions that do not place them at a significant disadvantage vis-à-vis their opponent (*Dombo Beheer BV v Netherlands* (1994)).

The emphasis placed by the Court on overriding fairness may be illustrated from *Asch v Austria* (1993), in which the Court held that there was no breach even where, on the face of it, there was a lack of compliance with one of the specific guarantees construed narrowly but there was fairness over the procedure as a whole. In that case, the applicant's domestic partner had complained that he assaulted her and there was medical evidence to show that she had sustained injuries consistent with that allegation. However, she subsequently returned to the police station to say that she and the applicant had been reconciled and that she had returned to live with him. She expressed her wish to withdraw her complaint. Despite this, the prosecutor proceeded with the case. She refused to give evidence and her statement was read out by a police officer. The applicant was convicted. The Court held that the guarantees in para.3 of art.6 are specific aspects of the right to a fair trial. Although the applicant's partner had refused to testify at the hearing she should, for the purposes of art.6.3(d), be regarded as a witness—a term to be given an autonomous interpretation—because her statements, as taken down in writing by a police officer and then related orally by him at the hearing, were, in fact, before the court, which took account of them. The Court considered that the admissibility of evidence is primarily a matter for regulation by national law and, as a rule, it is for the national courts to assess the evidence before them. The Court's task is to ascertain whether the proceedings considered as a whole, including the way in which evidence was taken, were fair. The Court said that all the evidence must normally be produced in the presence of the accused at a public hearing with a view to adversarial argument but that this does not mean that the statement of a witness must always be made in court and in public if it is to be admitted in evidence; in particular, this may prove impossible in certain cases. The use in this way of statements obtained at the pre-trial stage is not in itself inconsistent with paras 3(d) and 1 of art.6, provided that the rights of the defence have been respected. As a rule, these rights require that the accused be given an adequate and proper opportunity to challenge and question a witness against them, either when they were making their statements or at a later stage of the proceedings.

The Court thought that it would clearly have been preferable if it had been possible to hear the witness in person, but the right upon which she relied in order to avoid giving evidence could not be allowed to block the prosecution, the appropriateness of which it was not for the Court to determine. Subject to the rights of the defence being respected, it was therefore open to the national court to have regard to the statement, in particular in view of the fact that it could consider it to be corroborated by other evidence before it, including the two medical certificates attesting to the injuries.

Furthermore, the Court said, the applicant had the opportunity to discuss **6–04** his partner's version of events and to put his own, first to the police and later to the court. However, on each occasion he gave a different version, which tended to undermine his credibility. It was clear from the file that the partner's statements did not constitute the only item of evidence on which the first instance court based its decision. It also had regard to the personal assessment made by the police officer as a result of his interviews with the applicant and with his partner, to the two concurring medical certificates, to the police investigation and to the other evidence appearing in the applicant's file. The fact that it was impossible to question the lady at the hearing did not therefore, in the circumstances of the case, violate the rights of the defence and did not deprive the accused of a fair trial. Accordingly, there had been no breach of paras 1 and 3(d) of art.6, taken together.

At first, this result appears startling to British eyes. Article 6.3(d) reads like a guarantee of the right to cross-examine and that plainly was not afforded to the applicant. The approach of the Court, however, was to emphasise overall fairness and, finding no unfairness in what had happened, to find no breach of art.6.

It is also important to note that the Court said, in *Doorson v the Netherlands* (1996):

> "It is true that Article 6 does not explicitly require the interests of witnesses in general, and of those of victims called upon to testify in particular, to be taken into consideration. However, their life, liberty or security of person may be at stake, as may interests coming generally within the ambit of Article 8 of the Convention. Such interests of witnesses and victims are in principle protected by other, substantive provisions of the Convention, which imply that Contracting States should organise their criminal proceedings in such a way that those interests are not unjustifiably imperilled. Against this background, principles of fair trial also require that in appropriate cases the interests of the defence are balanced against those of witnesses and victims called upon to testify."

This may be seen in the context of the Court's earlier remark in *Soering v United Kingdom* (1989), that

> "inherent in the whole of the Convention is a search for a fair balance between the demands of the general interest of the community and the requirements of the protection of the individual's fundamental rights"

(a remark made in the context of art.3 of ECHR, which might well be the most absolute of the Convention rights).

The same principle, of fairness over the trial as a whole, arose in *Teixeira de Castro v Portugal* (1998). In that case, police officers hoped that through a drug addict and small time dealer they would be able to identify a more significant drug supplier. Unaware that they were police officers, the man agreed to find a supplier and mentioned the name of the applicant. A meeting eventually took place, at which the officers said that they wished to buy drugs. The applicant agreed to procure heroin and, through intermediaries, did so. The police officers then identified themselves and arrested the applicant, who was in due course convicted and sentenced to six years' imprisonment. He complained of a breach of art.6.

The Court analysed the matter primarily in terms of overall fairness rather than on the detailed wording of any part of art.6. It held that the use of undercover agents must be restricted and safeguards put in place even in cases concerning the fight against drug trafficking and that the public interest cannot justify the use of evidence obtained as a result of police incitement. On the facts of the particular case, the Court concluded that the two police officers' actions went beyond those of undercover agents because they instigated the offence and there was nothing to suggest that without their intervention it would have been committed. That intervention and its use in the impugned criminal proceedings meant that, from the outset, the applicant was deprived of a fair trial so that there had been a violation of art.6.1.

THE RIGHT TO A COURT

6–05 The first specific identifiable right in art.6.1 is the right to a hearing, sometimes called the "right to a court". We have already seen, from *Golder v United Kingdom*, that the Court rejected a government argument that art.6 regulates the conduct of the hearing but does not create a right to a hearing as such. Nevertheless, the right is not unlimited. It is, for example, not breached by the dismissal of an action on the ground of irrelevancy (*Whaley v Lord Advocate* (2008)) or by the operation of prescription (*Kelly v Gilmartin's Executrix* (2004)).

There is a right to a hearing in the determination of:
- civil rights and obligations; and
- criminal charges.

These concepts are autonomous and whether or not something is a matter of civil right or obligation or a criminal charge according to national law is of limited significance.

A number of cases before the Court and the Commission have made it clear that these categories are not unlimited but it is very difficult to extract principles of general applicability from the cases. The Court examines the particular circumstances of each dispute and comes to a conclusion after something of a balancing exercise taking into account all of the competing factors.

Civil rights and obligations

It can be said that matters within the category of private law, such as the law **6–06** of delict, family law or the law of property, will always constitute civil rights and obligations (see, for example, *Axen v Federal Republic of Germany* (1983); *Airey v Ireland* (1979–1980); *Buchholz v Federal Republic of Germany* (1980); and *Langborger v Sweden* (1989)). The relationship between the individual and the state, dealt with under the heading of public law, is likely to be a matter of civil right or obligation if the right in question is a pecuniary one (*Editions Périscope v France* (1992); *Stran Greek Refineries and Stratis Andreadis v Greece* (1994)). In *Schouten and Meldrum v the Netherlands* (1995) the Court said that there may exist "pecuniary" obligations vis-à-vis the state or its subordinate authorities which, for the purpose of art.6.1, are to be considered as belonging exclusively to the realm of public law and are accordingly not covered by the notion of "civil rights and obligations". The Court said that, apart from fines imposed by way of "criminal sanction", this will be the case, in particular, where an obligation which is pecuniary in nature derives from tax legislation or is otherwise part of normal civic duties in a democratic society. In that case, the Court then went on to conduct a detailed balancing exercise on whether Dutch social security contributions had more in common with tax or with insurance premiums. It concluded that insurance premiums were a closer analogy, so that art.6 did apply; but that conclusion depended on the particular nature of the Dutch scheme. *Application against Finland* (1995) is an example of a case which went in the other direction with the Commission holding that a dispute about a refusal to issue a passport was not within the scope of art.6.

Within the UK, it has been held (by English courts) that applications for sex offender orders and antisocial behaviour orders are civil proceedings for art.6 purposes (*B v Chief Constable of Avon and Somerset Constabulary* (2001); *R (McCann) v Manchester Crown Court* (2001)) but tax assessments are not (*Eagerpath Ltd v Edwards* (2001)). Nor are determinations of claims for accommodation under housing legislation (*Ali v Birmingham City Council* (2010)).

Criminal charge

The concept of the criminal charge is somewhat less complex. In *Engel*, **6–07** the Court noted in relation to military offences that all the contracting states make a distinction of long standing, albeit in different forms and degrees, between disciplinary proceedings and criminal proceedings. For the individuals affected, the former usually offer substantial advantages in comparison with the latter, for example, as concerns the sentences passed. Disciplinary sentences, in general less severe, do not appear in the person's criminal record and entail more limited consequences. The Court said that, in order to determine whether there is a criminal charge, for the purposes of art.6, it is necessary to know as a starting point whether the provision(s) defining the offence charged belong, according to the legal system of the respondent state, to criminal law, disciplinary law or both concurrently. The indications so afforded have only a formal and relative value and have then to be examined in the light of the common denominator of the respective legislation of the various contracting states. Then, the Court explained, the nature of the offence is a factor of greater import. When a serviceman finds himself accused of an act or omission allegedly contravening a legal rule governing the operation of the armed forces, the state may, in principle, employ against him disciplinary law rather than criminal law. But where the aim is the imposition of serious punishments involving deprivation of liberty the "charges" will come within the "criminal" sphere and art.6 will be applicable.

These rules were applied in *Öztürk v Federal Republic of Germany* (1984). The applicant had been dealt with in respect of a minor road traffic accident in which he was at fault and had been required to pay a rather modest administrative penalty of DM60. The German Government argued that art.6 did not apply to this procedure. However, the Court noted that, according to the ordinary meaning of the terms, there generally come within the ambit of the criminal law offences that make their perpetrator liable to penalties intended, inter alia, to be deterrent and usually consisting of fines and of measures depriving the person of his liberty. In addition, misconduct of the kind committed by Mr Öztürk continued to be classified as part of the criminal law in the vast majority of the contracting states, as it had been in the Federal Republic of Germany until the entry into force of the decriminalising legislation. Moreover, the changes related essentially to procedural matters and to the range of sanctions, which retained a punitive character, which is the customary distinguishing feature of criminal penalties. The rule of law infringed by the applicant had undergone no change of content. It was a rule that was directed, not towards a given group possessing a special status—in the manner, for example, of disciplinary law—but towards all citizens in their capacity as road users. The Court considered that the general character of the rule and the purpose of the penalty, being both deterrent and punitive, sufficed to show that the offence in question was, in terms of art.6 of the Convention, criminal in nature.

In *Hamer v Belgium* (2007), an order to demolish a house that had been built in breach of planning regulations was held to amount to a "penalty" such as to engage the criminal law aspect of art.6, even though there was no criminal conviction.

6–08   In *Öztürk*, the Court added that there is nothing to suggest that the criminal offence referred to in the Convention necessarily implies a certain degree of seriousness and that it would be contrary to the object and purpose of art.6, which guarantees to "everyone charged with a criminal offence" the right to a court and to a fair trial, if the state were allowed to remove from the scope of this article a whole category of offences merely on the ground of regarding them as petty.

The concept of the criminal charge is not limited to proceedings which take place in criminal courts. In *King v Walden (Inspector of Taxes)* (2001), it was held that a determination by a tax commissioner to penalise a defaulting taxpayer involved a criminal charge. In *Janosevic v Sweden* (2002), the Strasbourg Court found that certain tax surcharges could be considered to involve a "criminal charge" and so engage art.6. However, the criminal law aspect of art.6 is not engaged by the restrictions involved in an antisocial behaviour order (*R (McCann) v Manchester Crown Court* (2003)).

Article 6 does not apply to investigations under the Companies Acts, even though they have a quasi-judicial character (*Al-Fayed v United Kingdom* (1994)). Nor does it necessarily apply to prison disciplinary proceedings, even though they are in many ways analogous to criminal proceedings (*McFeeley v United Kingdom* (1980)). In some cases, however, examination of the particular prison proceedings will lead to the conclusion that they do amount to a criminal charge. In *Ezeh v United Kingdom; Connors v United Kingdom* (2002), both applicants had been convicted of prison disciplinary offences which had equivalents in ordinary criminal law. The Court found that the nature of the charges against the applicants, together with the nature and severity of the potential and actual penalties, were such as to lead to the conclusion that both applicants were subject to criminal charges.

PUBLIC HEARING

In the cases to which it applies, art.6 requires that the hearing should be in **6–09** public. In *Axen*, the Court said that the purpose of the guarantee of a public hearing is to protect litigants

> "against the administration of justice in secret with no public scrutiny; it is also one of the means whereby confidence in the courts, superior and inferior, can be maintained. By rendering the administration of justice visible, publicity contributes to the achievement of the aim of art.6.1, namely a fair trial".

The article goes on, however, to authorise the exclusion of the public and even of the press

> "in the interest of morals, public order or national security in a democratic society, where the interests of juveniles or the protection

of the private life of the parties so require, or to the extent strictly necessary in the opinion of the court in special circumstances where publicity would prejudice the interests of justice".

This part of art.6 has not been the subject of much consideration by the Strasbourg organs. There was comment in *Campbell and Fell v United Kingdom* (1985) that ordinary criminal proceedings nearly always take place in public, notwithstanding security problems; but this passage was descriptive and not normative. Moreover, the reference was made simply to draw a distinction between an ordinary trial and prison disciplinary proceedings (with which that case was concerned). In *X v Austria* (1965) the Commission approved the exclusion of the public from a trial for sexual offences against children, without identifying the reasoning which led to that conclusion; so the case scarcely goes beyond what is said in the plain words of the Convention. In *Monnell and Morris v United Kingdom* (1987) the Court held that a decision to grant or refuse of leave to appeal, the question being whether the appellant has demonstrated the existence of arguable grounds, was of such a limited nature as not to call for oral argument at a public hearing or the personal appearance of the prospective appellant. In *Martin v United Kingdom* (1999) the Court applied *Monnell and Morris* and held that an application which attacked the sifting of appeals by the High Court of Justiciary was manifestly ill founded.

HEARING WITHIN A REASONABLE TIME

6–10 Article 6.1 requires that the hearing should proceed "within a reasonable time". The purpose of this was said, in *Stögmüller v Austria* (1979–1980) to be to protect against excessive procedural delays. In criminal cases, the period to be taken into consideration commences when the accused has been charged, which generally means, for Convention purposes, the date when official notification is given to them by a competent authority that it is alleged that they have committed an offence, or the date from which their situation is substantially affected as a result of the suspicion against them (*Eckle v Germany* (1983)). It may sometimes take the form of other measures that carry the implication of such an allegation and that likewise substantially affect the situation of the subject (*Corigliano v Italy* (1982)). In some cases, this will be the date of arrest (*Wemhoff v Germany* (1979–1980)) but since the accused is not always arrested, in some cases another means of identifying the relevant stage must be sought. It is likely that the police, by cautioning and charging the accused, will start the clock running. It might be argued that the date on which the police first interview the accused as a suspect should be the date from which time is counted but the analysis made by Lord Hope of Craighead in the Supreme Court in *O'Neill v HM Advocate (No.2)* (2014) makes it clear that things are not that simple. Lord Hope explained that the point at which art.6 is engaged for the fair trial guarantee is not necessarily the same as the point for the reasonable time guarantee. In that case, the appellants were questioned as suspects in a murder investigation in 1998 but not charged on petition until 2005. Having examined the nature of the evidence available and the developing state of the investigation, Lord Hope concluded that it was only in 2005 that the reasonable time guarantee began to run.

In *Neumeister v Austria* (1979–1980) the applicant appeared for the first time as a suspect before an investigating judge on January 21, 1960. On that date he was interrogated and released. He was arrested and placed in detention on February 23, 1961 and the Court treated that as the date on which he had been charged. In *HM Advocate v McLean* (1999), the High Court of Justiciary rejected the proposition that actions by the Social Work Department and Reporter to the Childrens' Panel, taken without reference to the police or procurator fiscal, could "start the clock".

The period to be taken into account lasts until the determination of the charge and that includes any appeal (*Neumeister; Monnell and Morris*). Neither the Convention nor the Court has set out any absolute period of time within which proceedings must be completed if the requirement for trial within a reasonable time is to be met. Reasonableness will, the Court has said, always be a matter of particular circumstances (*König v Germany* (1980)). It seems clear too that, whilst the High Court of Justiciary is alert to the risk that concentrating on domestic standards would lead to art.6.1 being applied differently in different countries (with the perverse result that a breach is more likely to be found in countries with legal systems that are generally efficient), judges of the High Court will consider the circumstances of each case in light of their general knowledge of the Scottish criminal justice system. The Lord Justice General said as much in *HM Advocate v McGlinchey and Renicks* (2000). The approach taken by both the European Court and the High Court of Justiciary is to look first at the delay and then, if the time taken appears prima facie unreasonable, to require the state or the Crown (as the case may be) to explain the delay. In the case law of the Court, it is possible to identify three factors as important, these being:

- the complexity of the case;
- the conduct of the applicant; and
- the conduct of the authorities.

These factors are taken cumulatively. The Court makes its own assessment **6–11** of the reasonableness of the time in a given case (there is no margin of appreciation) but it does so having regard to the fact that art.6 can only require such expedition as is consistent with the proper administration of justice (*Stögmüller*). It has recognised as relevant to the criterion of complexity:

- the volume of evidence (*Eckle*);
- the number of accused persons or charges (*Neumeister*);
- the need to obtain expert evidence (*Wemhoff*);
- the need to obtain evidence from abroad (*Neumeister*); and
- the complexity of the legal issues involved (*Neumeister*).

These categories are not closed. In *HM Advocate v R* (2003), Lord Hope of Craighead said:

> "It is clear that the concept of reasonableness implies that a relatively high threshold must be crossed before it can be said in any particular case that a period of delay is unreasonable ... Among the factors to be taken into account in deciding where that threshold lies is the public interest ... A fair balance must be struck between the demands of the general interest of the community and the requirements of the protection of the individual's fundamental rights. But once that threshold has been crossed and it has been held that there has been a delay which is unreasonable within the meaning of the article, the position is irretrievable."

There is no generally "appropriate" time required, either for the police to report a matter to the procurator fiscal, or thereafter for any of the stages that lead to eventual indictment. Every case has to be examined on its own facts (*Gibson*). In line with the Strasbourg case law, complexity will be a relevant explanation for a longer period of preparation, as it was in *Crummock (Scotland) Ltd v HM Advocate* (2000). It is, however, the period as a whole that is important (*Smith v HM Advocate* (2000)); and it is not correct to adopt a piecemeal approach either by the defence criticising individual periods of inactivity in a case which as a whole proceeds within a reasonable time (*HM Advocate v McGlinchey and Renicks* (2000)) or by the Crown seeking to justify each individual chapter of the time taken in a case which, overall, has taken too long (*Kane v HM Advocate* (2001)).

Early Scots cases on the right in criminal cases to a hearing within a reasonable time proceeded on the basis that the remedy for breach was dismissal of the proceedings. In *Spiers v Ruddy* (2009), however, it was made clear that breach of this part of art.6 can be met by a reduction in sentence.

6–12   The right to a hearing within a reasonable time does not, in a case in which there is an insufficiency of evidence, preclude the prosecution authorities from keeping a file open against the possibility of a change in circumstances making it possible to proceed (*Robb v HM Advocate* (2000)).

It needs to be stressed that the entitlement to a hearing within a reasonable time is not confined to criminal cases. *Caillot v France* (1999) and *Nunes Violante v Portugal* (1999) both concerned the art.6.1 right to a hearing within a reasonable time in the determination of civil rights. In February 1990 the applicant in *Caillot* sought from the Tribunal Administratif of Caen an annulment of a decision of the commission charged with responsibility for land consolidations, which he regarded as being to his disadvantage. The proceedings were only concluded in May 1996, with a decision of the Conseil d'Etat—a delay of six years and three months. Three years and four months of that were attributable to the procedure in the Conseil d'Etat. The Government argued that this delay was not significant enough to amount to a breach of the Convention.

Nunes Violante concerned a claim from a union pension fund in respect of a work injury. It had already lasted over nine years and was still not resolved when the case was heard in Strasbourg. The Portuguese Government argued that this period did not constitute unreasonable delay but the judgment of the Court does not explain on what basis the Government maintained that position.

In both cases, the Court reiterated that whether or not a delay is reasonable will depend on the complexity of the issue, the conduct of the applicant and the conduct of the authorities. The cases in question were not complex and there were significant periods of inactivity. In *Caillot*, the Court said that it is incumbent on states to organise their judicial systems so as to guarantee to everyone the right to obtain a decision within a reasonable time. It did not consider that the time which elapsed while the case was in the Conseil d'Etat could be regarded as reasonable and awarded the applicant 25,000FF in just satisfaction. Nor did it regard the delay in *Nunes Violante* as reasonable and it awarded 800,000PTE with expenses.

The response of both France and Portugal in these cases seems to have consisted of little but an assertion that the period in question was not unreasonable. Whilst every case must be considered on its own facts, it is clear from *Eckle* that there comes a time when a delay becomes prima facie inordinate and it then falls to the respondent state to come forward with explanations.

INDEPENDENT AND IMPARTIAL TRIBUNAL

The next element particularly specified by art.6.1 is that the tribunal which **6–13** determines the charge should be independent and impartial and established by law. It should be noted that it is the ultimate determining tribunal that really matters (*Bryan v United Kingdom* (1995)). In *R v Secretary of State for the Environment, Transport and the Regions Ex p. Holding and Barnes Plc* (2001), the House of Lords held that the Secretary of State's power to "call in" a planning application does not offend against this part of art.6 because the Secretary of State's actions are subject to judicial review which ensures the compatibility of the overall procedure. This was followed in *County Properties v Scottish Ministers* (2001).

Security of tenure
The first aspect of this is that the judge should have reasonable security of **6–14** tenure, so as to protect them against undue influence. As the Commission put it in *Zand v Austria* (1978)

" ... according to the principles of the rule of law in democratic states which is the common heritage of the European countries, the irremovability of judges during their term of office, whether it be for a limited period of time or for lifetime, is a necessary corollary of their independence from the Administration and thus included in the guarantees of Article 6.1 of the Convention".

The particular judge

6–15 The other aspect of the guarantee relates to the particular judge in the case; and here we begin by considering *Pullar v United Kingdom* (1996) in which the applicant complained that he had not had a fair trial because one of jurors was employed by a prosecution witness.

The Court held that the view taken by the accused with regard to the impartiality of the tribunal could not be conclusive. What mattered was whether his doubts could be held to be objectively justified. Although the principle of impartiality is an important element in support of the confidence which the courts must inspire in a democratic society, the Court said that

> "it does not necessarily follow from the fact that a member of a tribunal has some personal knowledge of one of the witnesses in a case that he will be prejudiced in favour of that person's testimony. In each individual case it must be decided whether the familiarity in question is of such a nature and degree as to indicate a lack of impartiality on the part of the tribunal".

The Court took note of the fact that the employee was only one of 15 jurors, that the jury was directed to dispassionately assess the credibility of all the witnesses before them and that all of the jurors took an oath to similar effect. It held that there was no breach of art.6.1. A somewhat similar approach was taken in *Hauschildt v Denmark* (1989).

Pullar concerned the jury but contains material which is helpful in considering the position of the judge. The Court said in *Pullar* that

> "the principal that a tribunal shall be presumed to be free of prejudice or partiality is long established in the case law of the court".

This presumption is extremely strong and in fact, in the European jurisprudence, no claim of bias by a judge seems ever to have been successful. In *Piersack v Belgium* (1982), however, the Court did comment that a judge in respect of whom there was a legitimate reason to fear partiality must withdraw and this is of great practical significance. In attempting to formulate a test that would be in harmony with the Strasbourg case law, the House of Lords said, in *Porter v Magill* (2002) that the question is "whether the fair-minded and informed observer, having considered the facts, would conclude that there was a real possibility that the tribunal was biased" (Lord Hope).

6–16 In *Hoekstra v HM Advocate (No.2)* (2000), the publication by an appellate judge of a newspaper article, critical of the incorporation of ECHR into Scots law at a time when the appellant's appeal, based on ECHR, was current before an appellate bench which he chaired, was enough to justify the discharge of the bench. *CG v United Kingdom* (2002), dealing with an excessively interventionist trial judge, suggests, however, that the threshold may be quite high.

At one time, it was being suggested that the use of juries was incompatible with art.6 because they cannot give reasons for their decisions. That notion did not survive *Taxquet v Belgium* (2012) and *Judge v United Kingdom* (2011), in which it was held that the directions given to the jury, tailored as they should be to the particular case, can (and, in *Judge*, did) accomplish all that is needed.

It is worth noting here that the High Court was, in *Crummock (Scotland) Ltd v HM Advocate* (2000), unimpressed with the argument that a company charged with contaminating the Edinburgh water supply could not get a fair trial from an Edinburgh jury. However, for an example of jury irregularities that brought about a breach of art.6, see *Sander v United Kingdom* (2001).

Children's hearings were held to have the necessary independence in *S v Miller (No.1)* (2001).

ARTICLE 6.2

The presumption of innocence

The classic statement of the primary meaning of art.6.2 is to be found in **6–17** *Barberà, Messegué and Jabardo v Spain* (1989):

> "Paragraph 2 embodies the principle of the presumption of innocence. It requires, inter alia, that when carrying out their duties the members of a court should not start with the preconceived idea that the accused has committed the offence charged, and any doubt should benefit the accused."

Presumptions

The Court has also addressed presumptions under the heading of art.6.2. In **6–18** *Salabiaku v France* (1991), the court said that

> "presumptions of fact or of law operate in every legal system. Clearly the Convention does not prohibit such presumptions in principle. It does, however, require the Contracting States to remain within certain limits in this respect as regards criminal law ... It requires States to confine them within reasonable limits which take into account the importance of what is at stake and maintain the rights of the defence".

In *R v DPP Ex p. Kebilene* (2000), in relation to an argument about the reversal of the onus of proof, Lord Hope of Craighead distinguished between the shifting from the prosecution to the accused of the "evidential burden" (or the burden of introducing evidence in support of their case) on the one hand, and the "persuasive burden" (or the burden of persuading the jury as to their guilt or innocence) on the other. Statutory presumptions which place an "evidential" burden on the accused, requiring the accused to do no more than raise a reasonable doubt on the matter with which they deal, do not breach the presumption of innocence. In relation to statutory presumptions which transfer the "persuasive" burden to the accused, Lord Hope of Craighead stated that first, there is the "mandatory" presumption of guilt as to an essential element of the offence. As the presumption is one which must be applied if the basis of fact on which it rests is established, it is inconsistent with the presumption of innocence. Secondly, there is a presumption of guilt as to an essential element which is "discretionary". The tribunal of fact may or may not rely on the presumption, depending upon its view as to the cogency or weight of the evidence. If the presumption is of this kind it may be necessary for the facts of the case to be considered before a conclusion can be reached as to whether the presumption of innocence has been breached. In that event the matters cannot be resolved until after trial. The third category of provisions that fall within the general description of reverse onus clauses consists of provisions that relate to an exemption or proviso that the accused must establish if they wish to avoid conviction but is not an essential element of the offence. These provisions may or may not violate the presumption of innocence, depending on the circumstances. The provisions vary widely in their detail as to what the prosecutor must prove before the onus shifts, and their effect on the presumption of innocence depends highly on circumstances. These matters may not be capable of being fully assessed until after the trial.

R (on the application of International Transport Roth GmbH) v Secretary of State for the Home Department (2002) provides an example of a disproportionate reverse burden but *Glancy v HM Advocate* (2012), which deals with the statutory defence of reasonable excuse for having a bladed or sharply pointed item in a public place, is an example of a case in which the High Court of Justiciary analysed this aspect of art.6 in some detail and concluded that the reverse burden in relation to that matter was compatible with the Convention.

The right to silence
6–19 The Court has derived a right to silence from the presumption of innocence stipulated by art.6.2 but it held in *Murray v United Kingdom* (1996) that the right is not absolute. In that case the evidence against the applicant had been formidable. The Court said that

> "on the one hand it is self evident that it is incompatible with the immunities under consideration to base a conviction solely or mainly on the accused's silence or on a refusal to answer questions or to give evidence himself. On the other hand, the Court deems it equally obvious that these immunities cannot and should not prevent that the accused's silence, in situations which clearly call for an explanation from him, be taken into account in assessing the persuasiveness of evidence adduced by the prosecution".

Different considerations apply to compulsory powers to require answers to questions. It should be noted that there is a difference between the right to require answers and the use of those answers at trial (*R v Hertfordshire County Council Ex p. Green Environmental Industries* (2000)). In *Saunders v United Kingdom* (1996) a breach of art.6.2 was found where the prosecution made extensive use at trial of answers obtained from the accused under compulsory powers in ss.432 and 442 of the Companies Act 1985. With this case, there should be contrasted *Brown v Stott* (2001) in which the Privy Council held that art.6.2 is not absolute and that there was no breach of Convention rights inherent in the prosecutor leading in evidence, as regards a drink/driving prosecution, a reply to a requirement made by the police under s.172 of the Road Traffic Act 1988. That requirement was that a person suspected of such an offence should tell the police who was driving the car. The judicial committee noted that s.172 is restricted to serious offences (less serious and regulatory offences being excluded) and considered that the putting of a single question (refusal to answer which was visited with only moderate penalties) was a proportionate response to a serious social problem. *Brown* related to s.172(2)(a) but the reasoning was held, in *DPP v Wilson* (2001) to apply equally to s.172(2)(b). In *Attorney General's Reference (No.7 of 2000)* (2001), the Court of Appeal held that the use by the Crown in the prosecution of a bankrupt for an offence under the Insolvency Act of documents which were delivered up to the Official Receiver under compulsion but which do not contain statements made under compulsion is acceptable under art.6.1. *Heaney v Ireland* (2001) makes it clear, however, that information obtained under compulsory powers cannot always be used without a breach.

It should be noted that in *Saunders*, the Court pointed out, as commonly understood in the legal systems of the contracting parties to the Convention and elsewhere, the right to silence does not extend to the use in criminal proceedings of material which may be obtained from the accused through the use of compulsory powers but which has an existence independent of the will of the suspect such as, inter alia, documents acquired pursuant to a warrant, breath, blood and urine samples and bodily tissue for the purpose of DNA testing. This was applied in a drink/driving case in *Brown v Gallacher* (2002).

ARTICLE 6.3

Article 6.3 gives everyone charged with a criminal offence certain **6–20** minimum rights.

Information about the charge

Article 6.3(a) has on its face the following elements: **6–21**
- the accused must be informed of the nature and cause of the accusation;

- that information must be given promptly;
- that information must be detailed; and
- that information must be given in a language which the accused understands.

It is worth noting that, in *Bricmont v Belgium* (1986) the Commission said that the general purpose of this is to give the accused person the information they need to prepare their defence.

In *Gea Catalan v Spain* (1995) the Court approved of the Commission's interpretation of art.6.3(a). What the Commission said was that

> "the accused is entitled to be informed not only of the cause of the accusation, i.e. the material facts alleged against him which form the basis of the accusation, but also of the nature of the accusation, i.e. the legal classification of those material facts".

The circumstances in that case were that the applicant had taken advantage of his position as an employee of the Bank of Fomento to cause the bank to discount in his favour a number of bills of exchange which he had himself drawn, using false names. He was charged with obtaining property by deception as provided for in the Spanish Criminal Code. In pre-trial submissions the public prosecutor referred to a statutory aggravation of the offence but as a result of a typing error the reference given was to art.529(1) of the Criminal Code; it should have been to art.529(7). The applicant complained that he had not been informed of a component of the charge against him. The Court, however, held that the discrepancy complained of was clearly the result of a mere clerical error. It could not see how the applicant could complain that he had not been informed of all of the components of the charge since the prosecution case must have been obvious from its pre-trial submissions and since it should have been obvious that the aggravation provided for in art.529(1) had no application to the facts alleged but that art.529(7) did. It therefore held that there was no breach.

Next, the accused is entitled to be given the information "promptly". In *Application against Italy* (1988) the Commission held that the principal underlying purpose of the requirement for promptness, by which compliance will be judged, is to afford the accused time for the preparation of his defence.

6–22 In *Brozicek v Italy* (1990), the Court was satisfied with an indictment that specified date and place, listed the offences charged, referred to the relevant article of the Criminal Code and identified the victim.

Language is addressed by art.6.3(a) and translation by art.6.3(e). *Kamasinski v Austria* (1991) is relevant to both subparagraphs. In that case, the Court, whilst holding that the inadequacy of translation in the particular case did not in fact result in an unfair trial, did express clear views on the question of the translation of documents, including the indictment. So far as the general right to interpretation of documents is concerned, what they said was as follows:

"The right, stated in para.3(e) of art.6, to the free assistance of an interpreter applies not only to oral statements made at the trial hearing but also to documentary material and the pre-trial proceedings. Paragraph 3(e) signifies that a person 'charged with a criminal offence' who cannot understand or speak the language used in court has the right to the free assistance of an interpreter for the translation or interpretation of all those documents or statements in the proceedings instituted against him which it is necessary for him to understand or to have rendered into the court's language in order to have the benefit of a fair trial. However, para.3(e) does not go so far as to require a written translation of all items of written evidence or official documents in the procedure. The interpretative assistance provided should be such as to enable the defendant to understand the case against him and to defend himself, notably by being able to put before the court his version of events."

As regards the indictment in particular, the Court said that, whilst art.6.3(a)

"does not specify that the relevant information should be given in writing or translated in written form for a foreign defendant, it does point to the need for special attention to be paid to the notification of the 'accusation' to the defendant. An indictment plays a crucial role in the criminal process, in that it is from the moment of its service that the defendant is formally put on written notice of the factual and legal basis of the charges against him. A defendant not conversant with the court's language may in fact be put at a disadvantage if he is not also provided with a written translation of the indictment in a language he understands".

The Court did not hold, and has not held, that the provision of a written translation of the indictment will always be necessary to the fairness of the trial. In the *Kamasinski* case itself, the Court held that there was no unfairness despite the lack of such a translation. In so holding, they were influenced by a number of factors:
- the indictment was not complex;
- the applicant had been questioned at length by the police and investigating judges and must have been aware of the accusations levelled against him;
- notwithstanding the absence of a translation, the applicant had challenged the indictment on the ground of insufficiency of evidence;
- at no time did the applicant request that the indictment be translated; and
- when asked at the start of the trial, the applicant had told the trial court that he understood the charges.

Preparation for trial

6–23 Article 6.3(b) entitles the accused to adequate time and facilities for the preparation of his defence. According to Lord Hobhouse in *Buchanan v McLean* (2001):

> "The paragraph is principally directed to the securing for an accused person the opportunity and the services necessary for the preparation of his defence. It strikes at the imposition of restraints on his freedom to organise the preparation of his defence."

Lord Hobhouse gave as "an obvious example" a refusal of access to a lawyer while the accused is detained pending trial. In *Edwards* (1992), the Court said that it is a requirement of fairness that the prosecution authorities disclose to the defence all material evidence for or against the accused. That followed *Jespers v Belgium* (1982) in which the Commission said that

> "in any criminal proceedings brought by a state authority, the prosecution has at its disposal, to back the accusation, facilities deriving from its powers of investigation, supported by judicial and police machinery with considerable technical resources and means of coercion. It is in order to establish equality, as far as possible, between the prosecution and the defence that national legislation in most countries entrusts the preliminary investigation to a member of the judiciary or, if it entrusts the investigation to the Public Prosecutor's Department, instructs the latter to gather evidence in favour of the accused as well as evidence against him".

The Commission further took the view that the facilities to be provided should

> "include the opportunity to acquaint himself, for the purposes of preparing his defence, with the results of investigation carried out throughout the proceedings ... In short, Article 6, para.3(b) recognises the right of the accused to have at his disposal, for the purposes of exonerating himself or of obtaining a reduction in his sentence, all relevant elements that have been or could be collected by the competent authorities. The Commission considers that, if the element in question is a document, access to that document is a necessary 'facility' ... if, as in the present case, it concerns acts of which the defendant is accused, the credibility of testimony, etc.".

The Court said in *Kremzow v Austria* (1994) that restriction of the right to inspect the court file to an accused's lawyer is not incompatible with the rights of the defence under art.6.

Defence in person or through legal assistance

Article 6.3(c) entitles the accused to defend himself in person or through **6–24** legal assistance of his own choosing. Once a person is charged for art.6 purposes, that includes legal assistance before police questioning (*Ambrose v Harris* (2011)).

Trial in absence was said in *Poitrimol v France* (1994) not to be incompatible with the Convention in principle if the person concerned can subsequently obtain from a court which has heard him a fresh determination of the merits of the charge, in respect of both law and fact. The Court went on to say that it is open to question whether this latter requirement applies when the accused has waived his right to appear and to defend himself, but that at all events such a waiver must, if it is to be effective for Convention purposes, be established in an unequivocal manner and be attended by minimum safeguards commensurate with its importance. *R v O'Hare* (2006) is an example of a case in which repeated failures to appear or be represented were held to constitute such a waiver.

As to legal assistance of his own choosing, in *Croissant v Germany* (1993), the accused person had appointed lawyers whose places of business were geographically remote from the trial court, with the result that adjournments were likely. In order to avoid that, the trial court appointed a further defence lawyer who practised in the same city as the court. The accused person complained of a breach of art.6.3(c) but the Court found against him. It said that

> "notwithstanding the importance of a relationship of confidence between lawyer and client, this right cannot be considered to be absolute. It is necessarily subject to certain limitations where legal aid is concerned and also where, as in the present case, it is for the courts to decide whether the interests of justice require that the accused be defended by counsel appointed by them. When appointing defence counsel the national courts must certainly have regard to the defendant's wishes ... However, they can over-ride those wishes when there are relevant and sufficient grounds for holding that this is necessary in the interests of justice".

Examining witnesses

Article 6.3(d) provides, so far as relevant, that the accused is entitled to **6–25** "have examined the witnesses against him". The UK lawyer would read that and tend to take the view that hearsay is absolutely excluded. Support for that position would be derived from a superficial reading of *Unterpertinger v Austria* (1991), in which the applicant had been accused of assault upon his wife and stepdaughter. They had made statements to the police but declined to give evidence. He was convicted on the basis of the statements given to the police. The Court delivered a short judgement. The starting point was that

> "the reading out of statements in this way cannot be regarded as being

inconsistent with Article 6.1 and 3(d) of the Convention, but the use made of them as evidence must nevertheless comply with the rights of the defence, which it is the object and purpose of Article 6 to protect. This is especially so where the person 'charged with a criminal offence', who has the right under Article 6.3(d) to 'examine or have examined' witnesses against him, has not had an opportunity at any stage in the earlier proceedings to question the persons whose statements are read out at the hearing".

The conviction had been based "mainly" on the statements made by the wife and stepdaughter, which the Austrian court had treated as proof of the truth of the accusations rather than merely as what the Court referred to as "information". In these circumstances, it was held, the applicant's defence rights had been "appreciably restricted" so that he had not had a fair trial. The Strasbourg Court held that there had been a breach of art.6.1 taken with "the principles inherent in paragraph 3(d)"; but it is significant that the Court said that the reading out of statements was not in itself inconsistent with the Convention.

The Court went further in *Asch* (1993) holding that there had been no breach where the conviction was based in part upon the statement given to the police by the complainer in the case, who was the applicant's domestic partner and who had refused to give evidence at trial. However, it was of importance in that case that the evidence of the complainer was not the only evidence in the case. The police had observed injuries to the complainer and there was, in addition, medical evidence (though it does not seem to have addressed the identity of the assailant). It was also of importance that the applicant, when interviewed, had given several conflicting accounts of how the complainer came by her injuries which, the Court said, "tended to undermine his credibility".

6–26   In *Vickers v Buchanan* (2002), the High Court said that the guarantee

"cannot be taken to be entitling the accused to insist on the services of a particular individual irrespective of that individual's availability or, indeed, willingness to act. It is commonplace that accused persons, like litigants, might prefer to engage the services of a particular individual; but the exigencies of court timetabling and the practice of the particular individual in question may make it impossible for them to exercise that choice ... the content of the right must be that the accused is entitled to select from among the practitioners available, qualified and willing to act in the particular circumstances. Any other interpretation would entitle the accused to disrupt the business of the courts in an unacceptable way by insisting on being represented by a particular individual".

Special considerations apply in cases concerning sexual offences, especially those involving child victims, as the Court made clear in *SN v Sweden* (2004). The applicant was accused of the sexual abuse of a 10 year old boy, known as "M". A police interview with M took place and was recorded. On SN's request, the police carried out another recorded interview with M a few months later. The applicant's counsel did not attend, but indicated to the police officer who conducted the interview which issues needed to be addressed. The applicant was then indicted for sexual acts with a child. The trial court played the recordings of the child's interviews at the trial. Relying almost entirely on the child's assertions, the court convicted the applicant. The Court said that criminal proceedings in respect of sexual offences are often conceived of as an ordeal by the victim, especially when unwillingly confronted with the defendant. These features, it said, are even more prominent in a case involving a minor. In a critically important passage, the Court said that

> "the assessment of the question whether or not in such proceedings an accused received a fair trial, account must be taken of the right to respect for the private life of the perceived victim. Therefore, the Court accepts that in criminal proceedings concerning sexual abuse certain measures may be taken for the purpose of protecting the victim, provided that such measures can be reconciled with an adequate and effective exercise of the rights of the defence ... In securing the rights of the defence, the judicial authorities may be required to take measures which counterbalance the handicaps under which the defence labours".

Against this background, the Court said that art.6.3 cannot be interpreted as requiring in all cases that questions be put directly by the accused or their defence counsel, through cross-examination or by other means. It said that, while all evidence must normally be produced in the presence of the accused at a public hearing with a view to adversarial argument, the use in evidence of statements obtained at the stage of the police inquiry and the judicial investigation is not in itself inconsistent with art.6.1 and 3(d), provided that the rights of the defence have been respected. Explaining the concept of respecting the rights of the defence, the Court said that, as a rule, the defendant must be given an adequate and proper opportunity to challenge and question a witness against them, either when they were making their statements or at a later stage of the proceedings. Since in the applicant's case the statements made by M were virtually the sole evidence on which the courts' findings of guilt were based, it was for consideration whether the applicant was provided with an adequate opportunity to exercise his defence rights within the meaning of art.6 in respect of the evidence given by M. The Court decided that he had been provided with an adequate opportunity and based that assessment on two considerations. First, it was clear that the applicant's counsel had been able to have questions put to M by the police officer conducting the interview. Having subsequently listened to the audio tape and read the transcript of the interview, counsel for the applicant was apparently satisfied that the questions he had indicated to the police officer had actually been put to M.

Second, it was clear that the trial court and the appeal court had both given special consideration to the fact that M had not given evidence in court and had taken that into account in assessing his credibility.

Interpreters
For material on art.6.3(e), see the consideration of *Kamasinski* at para.6–22, above.

7. PROHIBITION OF RETROSPECTIVE CRIMINALISATION (ARTICLE 7)

INTRODUCTION

Article 7 is concerned exclusively with criminal law. It provides: 7–01

> 1. No one shall be held guilty of any criminal offence on account of any act or omission which did not constitute a criminal offence under national or international law at the time when it was committed. Nor shall a heavier penalty be imposed than the one that was applicable at the time the criminal offence was committed.

> 2. This article shall not prejudice the trial and punishment of any person for any act or omission which, at the time when it was committed, was criminal according to the general principles of law recognised by civilised nations.

In *Kokkinakis v Greece* (1994), the Strasbourg Court said that art.7.1

> "embodies ... the principle that only the law can define a crime and prescribe a penalty (*nullum crimen, nulla poena sine lege*) and the principle that the criminal law must not be extensively construed to an accused's detriment, for instance, by analogy; it follows from this that an offence must be clearly defined in law. This condition is satisfied where the individual can know from the wording of the relevant provision and, if need be, with the assistance of the court's interpretation of it, what acts and omissions will make him liable".

COMMON LAW AND ARTICLE 7

The Commission has treated common law offences as unobjectionable in 7–02 themselves but has made a distinction between that which clarifies the law and that which extends it such that it is made to "cover facts which previously clearly did not constitute a criminal offence" (*X Ltd and Y Ltd v United Kingdom* (1982)). As regards clarification, the Commission has said in the same case that

> "it is not objectionable that the existing elements of the offence are clarified and adapted to new circumstances which can reasonable be brought under the original conception of the offence".

In *SW and CR v United Kingdom* (1996), the Court recalled the words used in *Kokkinakis* and said that from those principles it followed that an offence must be clearly defined in the law. This requirement is satisfied where the individual can know from the wording of the relevant provision and, if need be, with the assistance of the courts' interpretation of it, what acts and omissions will make him criminally liable. The Court thus indicated that when speaking of "law" art.7 alludes to the same concept as that to which the Convention refers elsewhere when using that term, a concept which comprises written as well as unwritten law and implies qualitative requirements, notably those of accessibility and foreseeability. The Court pointed out that however clearly drafted a legal provision may be, in any system of law, including criminal law, there is an inevitable element of judicial interpretation. There will always be a need for elucidation of doubtful points and for adaptation to changing circumstances. Indeed, in the UK, as in the other convention states, the progressive development of the criminal law through judicial law-making is a well entrenched and necessary part of legal tradition. Article 7 of the Convention cannot be read as outlawing the gradual clarification of the rules of criminal liability through judicial interpretation from case to case, provided that the resultant development is consistent with the essence of the offence and could reasonably be foreseen. The Court considered that it could reasonably be foreseen that there would be judicial recognition of the absence of immunity on the part of a husband and commented too that the essentially debasing character of rape is so manifest that the result could not be said to be at variance with the object and purpose of art.7 of the Convention, namely to ensure that no one should be subjected to arbitrary prosecution, conviction or punishment. What was more, the abandonment of the unacceptable idea of a husband being immune against prosecution for rape of his wife was in conformity not only with a civilised concept of marriage but also, and above all, with the fundamental objectives of the Convention, the very essence of which is respect for human dignity and human freedom.

PENALTY

7–03 The issue of the imposition of a heavier penalty than that available at the time of the offence was considered in *Welch v United Kingdom* (1995). The applicant was arrested and charged in November 1986 in relation to drug trafficking offences. In January 1987 the Drug Trafficking Offences Act 1986 ("the 1986 Act") came into force, making it possible for the first time for English courts to impose confiscation orders. In February and May 1987 the applicant was charged with further drug trafficking offences. In August 1988 he was convicted of five counts. He was imprisoned and a confiscation order was imposed in the sum of £66,914 (subsequently reduced on appeal to £59,914). He complained under art.7 that the imposition of a confiscation order constituted a retroactive criminal penalty. The Government argued that the true purpose of a confiscation order was two-fold: first, to deprive a person of the profits he had received from drug trafficking; and second, to remove the value of the proceeds from future use in the drugs trade. On this basis, the Government argued, confiscation was not a penalty. The Court, held, however, that the concept of a penalty in art.7 is an autonomous Convention concept. The wording of art.7.1 indicates that the starting point for the assessment of the existence of a penalty is whether the measure is imposed following conviction for a criminal offence. Other factors that may be taken into account are the nature and purpose of the measure in question, its characterisation under national law, the procedures involved in the making and implementation of the measure and its severity. These factors are, of course, familiar from consideration of the term "criminal charge" in relation to art.6.

The Court noted that, before a confiscation order could be made in English law, the accused must have been convicted of a drug trafficking offence. This link is not diminished by the fact that, due to the operation of the statutory presumptions concerning the extent to which the accused has benefited from drug trafficking, the court order may affect proceeds which are not directly related to the facts underlying the criminal conviction. The 1986 Act was introduced to overcome the inadequacy of existing powers of forfeiture. Although the provisions were designed to ensure that proceeds were not available for use in future drug trafficking and that crime does not pay, the legislation also pursued the aim of punishing the offender. The aims of prevention and reparation are consistent with a punitive purpose and may be seen as constituent elements of the very notion of punishment.

Several aspects of the making of an order under the 1986 Act were in keeping with the idea of a penalty even though they were essential to the preventive scheme inherent in the 1986 Act (and are now to be found in the Proceeds of Crime Act 2002). These included the sweeping statutory assumptions that all property passing through the offender's hands during a six year period is the fruit of drug trafficking unless he can prove otherwise, the fact that the confiscation order is directed to proceeds and not restricted to actual enrichment or profit, the discretion the trial judge had under the 1986 Act in fixing the order to take account of the degree of culpability of the accused and the possibility of imprisonment in default of payment. These elements, considered together, provided a strong indication of inter alia a regime of punishment. Looking behind appearances at the reality of the situation, whatever the characterisation of the measure of confiscation, the fact remained that the applicant faced more far reaching detriment as a result of the order than that to which he was exposed at the time of the commission of the offences of which he was convicted. There was therefore a breach of art.7; but the Court stressed that its conclusion related only to the retrospective application of the legislation and did not call into question in any respect the powers of confiscation conferred on the courts as a weapon in the fight against the scourge of drug trafficking.

INTERNATIONAL LAW AND GENERAL PRINCIPLES OF LAW

7–04 The references in art.7.2 to offences under international law and to things that are criminal according to the general principles of law recognised by civilised nations have not been considered by the Court. However, in terms of international law, very few offences are within these categories. Piracy, slavery, genocide and the waging of a war of aggression are certainly within the categories and torture probably is (*R v Bow Street Metropolitan Stipendiary Magistrate Ex p. Pinochet Ugarte (No.3)* (1999)).

8. RIGHT TO RESPECT FOR PRIVATE LIFE (ARTICLE 8)

INTRODUCTION

Article 8 provides: **8–01**

> 1. Everyone has the right to respect for his private and family life, his home and his correspondence.
>
> 2. There shall be no interference by a public authority with the exercise of this right except such as is in accordance with the law and is necessary in a democratic society in the interests of national security, public safety or the economic well-being of the country, for the prevention of disorder or crime, for the protection of health or morals, or for the protection of the rights and freedoms of others.

This has been one of the most dynamically interpreted provisions of ECHR and it has an extremely wide application. *Johnston v Ireland* (1987) makes it clear that art.8 has relevance to family law. However, we shall see in a moment that its scope is far wider than merely family law (though one limitation is that the right cannot be claimed by a company—*R v Broadcasting Standards Commission Ex p. British Broadcasting Corporation* (2000)). First, we deal with the structure of art.8, which follows a pattern common to many of the Convention rights in that it states a right and then states the circumstances in which interference with the right may be permitted.

THE STRUCTURE OF ARTICLE 8

Paragraph 1 and the opening words of para.2 state the right: in this case, the **8–02** right to respect for private and family life, home and correspondence and the prohibition on interference with the right. Paragraph 2 then effectively qualifies this, stating the circumstances in which interference with the right may be permitted. In *Funke v France* (1993), the Court said that the exceptions provided for by art.8.2 are to be interpreted narrowly. Under art.8.2, before interference with the right is permitted it must, first, be in accordance with the law. Secondly, it must be necessary. Thirdly, it must be in pursuit of one of the specified objectives.

On reading the cases, it becomes very clear that the Court analyses art.8 issues within a well established framework which consists of five questions:

- Is the right relevant to what has happened?
- Is there an interference with the right?

- Is the interference in accordance with law?
- Does the interference pursue one of the permitted objectives?
- Is the interference necessary? This question has two parts. First, the Court asks if there was a "pressing social need" for the interference. Secondly, it asks whether what was done was proportionate to the need.

THE INTERESTS PROTECTED

8–03 The first question, then, is whether the right is relevant at all. It will be seen that there are four areas which are protected (though they will sometimes overlap). They are:
- private life;
- family life;
- home; and
- correspondence.

The core meanings of these phrases are clear enough; but they have all, to a greater or lesser extent, attracted extended meanings.

Private life
8–04 In *X and Y v the Netherlands* (1985) the Court said that the concept of the private life covers the physical and moral integrity of the person, including their sexual life (which was the aspect at issue in that case). Within that sphere, if the applicant had a reasonable expectation of privacy, they will be successful in establishing that art.8 is relevant.

Whether such an expectation existed and was reasonable will, of course, be questions to be assessed on the facts of the individual case. In *Halford v United Kingdom* (1997) the applicant was held to have had a reasonable expectation of privacy for telephone calls from her office, especially because one of her office phones was specifically designated for her private use and because she had been given an assurance that she could use her office telephones for the purposes of the sex discrimination case which she was pursuing against her employers (a police force). In *Peev v Bulgaria* (2007) the Court held that a public official could reasonably have expected his workspace—or at least his desk and filing cabinets in which he kept his personal belongings—to be treated as private property. Accordingly, a search amounted to an interference with his private life. By contrast, in *Friedl v Austria* (1995) it was held that a person taking part in a demonstration in a public place has no reasonable expectation of privacy (the complaint was that the police had taken the applicant's photograph). In *Connor v HM Advocate* (2002), the High Court held that observation of a public street and the door to a common close was not a breach of art.8. The Court of Appeal held in *R v Broadcasting Standards Commission Ex p. British Broadcasting Corporation* (2000), that in the absence of an element of seclusion, surreptitious filming in public was not an infringement of privacy. One may contrast *Peck v United Kingdom* (2003), in which it was held that the release by a local authority of CCTV footage to broadcasters did breach art.8 as regards a person who was the subject of the film. He had been in possession of a knife which he went on to use to cut his wrists. The Strasbourg Court considered that, following disclosure of the material to the media, the applicant's actions were seen to an extent which far exceeded any exposure to a passer-by, security observation and to a degree surpassing that which he could reasonably have foreseen. Again, whilst the Court was entirely satisfied that persons of homosexual orientation serving in the British armed forces had a reasonable expectation of privacy as regards their sexual practices (*Lustig-Prean and Beckett and Smith and Grady v United Kingdom* (2000)) it regarded it as seriously open to question whether the same could be said of a group of up to 44 men who engaged in sado-masochistic practices (involving the inflicting of injuries) with each other, video recording the proceedings and distributing those recordings within the group (*Laskey, Jaggard and Brown v UK* (1997)).

In *Pretty v United Kingdom* (2002), the Court said that the notion of personal autonomy is an important principle underlying the interpretation of art.8 and also that it is under art.8 that notions of quality of life take on significance.

As regards sexual identity, in *Goodwin v United Kingdom* (2002), the Court held that it was a breach of art.8 to refuse to give official recognition to the change effected by gender reassignment surgery.

Family

The existence or otherwise of a family life is primarily a question of fact, **8–05** which depends on the existence of close personal ties. In *Gas and Dubois v France* (2010), it applied to a homosexual couple raising a child conceived by artificial insemination with sperm from an anonymous donor. In *Moretti and Benedetti v Italy* (2010), it applied to the relationship between a host family and a foster child (art.8).

Home

"Home" is not a concept which is limited to the place where the applicant **8–06** is actually living at any given time. In *Gillow v United Kingdom* (1986), the applicants owned a house on Guernsey to which they always intended to return and kept their furniture in it. Since the first applicant's work required them to live elsewhere, they let the house to tenants over a period of almost 19 years. When they moved back to the house, the first applicant was prosecuted for breach of housing legislation which restricted the categories of persons entitled to live on the island. The Court held that, although the applicants had not lived in the house for 19 years, they had in fact retained sufficient continuing links with it for it to be considered their "home", for the purposes of art.8.

"Home" need not even be a house. In *Niemietz v Germany* (1992), which concerned the search by the police of a lawyer's office, the Court noted that in certain contracting states the concept of the "home" had been accepted as extending to business premises and that such an interpretation was fully consonant with the French text, since the word "domicile" has a broader connotation than the word "home" and may extend, for example, to a professional person's office. More generally, the Court considered, to interpret the words "private life" and "home" as including certain professional or business activities or premises would be consonant with the essential object and purpose of art.8, namely to protect the individual against arbitrary interference by the public authorities.

Correspondence

8–07 Correspondence plainly covers letters. In *Campbell v United Kingdom* (1992) there was a breach of art.8 where prison authorities opened and read letters between a prisoner and, amongst others, the European Commission on Human Rights. But it also covers telephone calls (*Halford* (1997); *Malone v United Kingdom* (1984)) and there does not seem to be any reason why it should not extend to other methods of communication, such as email.

INTERFERENCE

8–08 Given that one of the interests protected by art.8 is relevant, the next question is whether there is an interference with the right. In many cases, the answer will be obvious. Tapping telephones will amount to an interference (*Halford* (1997); *Malone* (1984)); so will searching a house or office (*Funke* (1993); *Niemitz* (1992)). In *Keegan* the secret placing of a child for adoption, so severing any possible link with the father (who was separated from the mother) was an interference. In *Principal Reporter v K* (2011) the exclusion of an unmarried father from proceedings before the children's hearing and the sheriff, which resulted in an order prohibiting contact between him and the child, constituted an interference with both his art.8 rights and those of the child.

It would be possible to multiply endless examples. What is less obvious, however, is the fact that it is enough if a state of affairs exists which puts an applicant's art.8 interests at risk. In *Norris v Ireland* (1991) the applicant was described as "an active homosexual" and a campaigner for homosexual rights. He objected in particular to the existence in Ireland of laws which made certain homosexual practices between consenting adult men criminal offences. Although prosecutions had been confined in practice to cases involving minors, there was no bar to prosecution in the case of such consenting adults. The Court held that, since there was a possibility of prosecution, the maintenance in force of the legislation constituted a continuing interference with the applicant's right to respect for his private life.

JUSTIFICATION FOR INTERFERENCE

Introduction

If it is established that art.8 is relevant to whatever has happened and that **8–09**
there has been an interference with the right which it guarantees, there will
be a breach of the article unless the respondent state establishes that the
criteria set out in art.8.2 are met.

Accordance with law

The first criterion is that the interference was in accordance with law. In **8–10**
Malone the Court explained that the phrase "in accordance with the law"
does not merely refer back to domestic law but also relates to the quality
of the law, requiring it to be compatible with the rule of law, which is
expressly mentioned in the preamble to the Convention. The phrase thus
implies that there must be a measure of legal protection in domestic law
against arbitrary interferences by public authorities with the rights
safeguarded by art.8.1. The position was made still clearer in *Khan v United
Kingdom* (2000). In that case, police officers investigating an allegation of
drug trafficking against certain persons including the applicant had installed
a listening device in a house occupied by one of those persons. The
installation was not in accordance with any rule of law but neither was it
prohibited by any rule of law. Tape recorded conversations obtained by
using that listening device constituted the totality of the prosecution case
against the applicant. He objected to the admissibility of the evidence of the
tape recordings but the trial judge declined to exclude the evidence under
s.78 of the Police and Criminal Evidence Act 1984 and the applicant
thereafter pled guilty, whereupon he was sentenced to a period of
imprisonment.

Before the Court it was conceded by the UK Government that the use of
a covert listening device in this way amounted to an interference with the
right to respect for private life guaranteed by art.8.1 of the Convention.
Rejecting the UK's submission that the existence of Home Office
guidelines to govern surveillance of this sort, constituted the necessary
"law" for the purposes of art.8.2, the Court noted that, since such guidelines
were neither legally binding nor directly publicly accessible, there was no
domestic law regulating the use of covert listening devices at the relevant
time and held that the interference could not, therefore, be considered to be
"in accordance with law" as required by art.8.2. There was, therefore, a
breach of art.8 and it was not necessary for the court to go further and
consider whether the interference was necessary and pursued one of the
specified legitimate aims. The Regulation of Investigatory Powers Act 2000
and the Regulation of Investigatory Powers (Scotland) Act 2000 were, in
large measure, responses to *Khan* and seek to provide the positive legal
framework that was previously lacking.

Legitimate aim

8–11 Assuming that the state establishes that whatever was done was in accordance with law, the next question will be whether it pursued one of the specified legitimate aims. It will be recalled that the Court said in *Funke* (1993) that these aims are exhaustive and to be construed narrowly.

Necessary

8–12 Although the question of necessity appears in art.8.2 before that of legitimate aim, it is frequently considered last by the Court. That is because it is often the most complex and finely balanced question in any art.8 case.

In *Dudgeon v United Kingdom* (1981) it was explained that "necessary" in the context of art.8 does not have the flexibility of such expressions as "useful", "reasonable", or "desirable", but implies the existence of a "pressing social need" for the interference in question. The Court said that it is for the national authorities to make the initial assessment of the pressing social need in each case and accordingly, a margin of appreciation is left to them.

In *Lustig-Prean and Beckett v United Kingdom* (2000) the state overstepped the mark. The applicants had both served in the Royal Navy but had been dismissed on account of their homosexuality. Prior to the discovery of their sexual orientation, both had received highly complimentary reports on their performance. When their sexual orientation came to the attention of the naval authorities, investigations were commenced and both applicants were interviewed. At those interviews they both acknowledged their homosexuality but the interviews continued and the second applicant in particular was asked highly detailed questions about his sexual practices. The applicants complained that the investigations into their sexual orientation and their subsequent discharge from the Royal Navy on the sole ground that they were homosexual, in pursuance of the Ministry of Defence's then absolute policy against homosexuals in the British armed forces, constituted a violation of their right to respect for their private lives protected by art.8 of the Convention.

The Court reiterated that an interference would be considered "necessary in a democratic society" for a legitimate aim if it answered a pressing social need and, in particular, was proportionate to the legitimate aim pursued. Given the matters at issue in the present case, the Court underlined the link between the notion of "necessity" and that of a "democratic society", the hallmarks of the latter including pluralism, tolerance and broadmindedness. The Court said that when the relevant restrictions concern a most intimate part of an individual's private life, there must exist particularly serious reasons before such interferences can satisfy the requirements of art.8.2 of the Convention. The core argument of the Government in support of the policy of dismissal was that the presence of open or suspected homosexuals in the armed forces would have a substantial and negative effect on morale and, consequently, on the fighting power and operational effectiveness of the armed forces. The Court found, however, that the perceived problems were founded solely upon the negative attitudes of heterosexual personnel towards those of homosexual orientation. The Court noted the lack of concrete evidence to substantiate the alleged damage to morale and fighting power that any change in the policy would entail. The Court considered it reasonable to assume that some difficulties could be anticipated as a result of any change in policy but was of the view that it had not been shown that conduct codes and disciplinary rules could not adequately deal with any behavioural issues arising. Accordingly, the Court concluded that convincing and weighty reasons had not been offered by the Government to justify the policy against homosexuals in the armed forces or, therefore, the consequent discharge of the applicants from those forces. In sum, the Court found that neither the investigations conducted into the applicants' sexual orientation, nor their discharge on the grounds of that orientation in pursuance of the Ministry of Defence policy, were justified under art.8.2 of the Convention.

Proportionality

In *Lustig-Prean* the Court referred to the question of proportionality. That **8–13** issue has been a consistent feature of the case law on art.8 (and other articles). What is meant is that, if an interference is to be regarded as necessary, it must be proportionate to the aim that it has sought to achieve. Lack of proportionality was the basis of the decision in *McLeod v United Kingdom* (1999). In that case, in connection with divorce proceedings, the applicant was ordered by a county court to deliver to her ex-husband a number of items and furniture from the former matrimonial home, where she lived with her elderly mother. The ex-husband arrived at the former matrimonial home, accompanied by his brother and sister and a solicitor's clerk. Fearing that there would be a breach of the peace because of Mrs McLeod's previous unwillingness to comply with orders of the court, her ex-husband's solicitors had arranged for two police officers to be present while the property was being removed. Mrs McLeod was not at home when her ex-husband and his party arrived. Her mother allowed them to enter the house and remove property. When the applicant returned home, she objected to the removal of the property. One of the police officers intervened and insisted that she allow her former husband to leave with the property. The Court considered that the police could not be faulted for responding to the solicitors' request for assistance, since there had been a genuine fear that a breach of the peace might occur when Mr McLeod removed his property from the former matrimonial home but considered that as soon as it became apparent that Mrs McLeod was not at home, the officers should not have entered the house, since it should have been clear to them that there was little or no risk of disorder or crime occurring. On these grounds, the Court found that the officers' entry had been disproportionate to the legitimate aim pursued and that there had been a violation of art.8 of the Convention.

In *Manchester City Council v Pinnock* (2010) the Supreme Court held **8–14** that a court which is asked to make an order for eviction from a council house needs to have power to assess proportionality if the procedure is to comply with art.8.

POSITIVE OBLIGATIONS

8–15 We have seen in Ch.1 that some of the articles of the Convention carry with them positive obligations. That was illustrated in Ch.1 by reference to *López Ostra* and further examples are to be found in *Marckx v Belgium* (1979–1980) and *X and Y v the Netherlands* (1985).

In *Marckx*, the applicants were a journalist and her illegitimate daughter. Under Belgian law, no legal bond between an unmarried mother and her child resulted from the mere fact of birth. Whilst the birth certificate recorded at the register office sufficed to prove the maternal affiliation of a married woman's children, the maternal affiliation of an illegitimate child required further procedure before it was established. The establishment of maternal affiliation had certain consequences for the extent of the child's family relationships and consequent rights of access and maintenance, and for her inheritance rights. To place the child on the same footing as a legitimate child, the mother had to adopt her. The Court held that by proclaiming the right to respect for family life, art.8 imposes a positive obligation on the state to act in a manner calculated to allow those concerned to lead a normal family life. Respect for family life implies in particular the existence in domestic law of legal safeguards that render possible, from the moment of birth, the child's integration in its family—which the particular legal regime applicable in the case failed to do.

In *X and Y v the Netherlands*, the second applicant was mentally handicapped and had been living in a privately-run home for mentally handicapped children. On the night after her 16th birthday a relative of a member of staff forced the girl to follow him to his room, to undress and to have sexual intercourse with him. The incident had traumatic consequences for her, causing her major mental disturbance. When he found out what had happened, her father (the first applicant) went to the local police station to file a complaint and to ask for criminal proceedings to be instituted. Rape could not be proved. There was an offence which applied to a person who

> "through gifts or promises ... through abuse of a dominant position resulting from factual circumstances, or through deceit, deliberately causes a minor of blameless conduct to commit indecent acts with him or to suffer such acts from him"

but in case of that kind, the offender could be prosecuted only on complaint by the actual victim. The victim, being mentally handicapped, was unable to make such a complaint and there could therefore be no prosecution.

8–16 The Court recalled that although the object of art.8 is essentially that of protecting the individual against arbitrary interference by the public authorities, it does not merely compel the state to abstain from such interference: in addition to this primarily negative undertaking, there may be positive obligations inherent in an effective respect for private or family life. These obligations, it said, may involve the adoption of measures designed to secure respect for private life even in the sphere of the relations of individuals between themselves. The choice of the means calculated to secure compliance with art.8 in the sphere of the relations of individuals between themselves is in principle a matter that falls within the contracting states' margin of appreciation. In this connection, there are different ways of ensuring "respect for private life", and the nature of the state's obligation will depend on the particular aspect of private life that is at issue. Recourse to the criminal law is not necessarily the only answer. However, the protection afforded by the civil law in the case of wrongdoing of the kind inflicted on the second applicant was insufficient. This was a case where fundamental values and essential aspects of private life were at stake. Effective deterrence was indispensable in this area and it could be achieved only by criminal law provisions. Since the law did not provide the second applicant with practical and effective protection, it had to be concluded, taking account of the nature of the wrongdoing in question, that she was the victim of a violation of art.8.

The Court reached the same result in *Söderman v Sweden* (2013), in which the applicant's stepfather was prosecuted for attempting to film her naked in the bathroom of her home when she was 14 years old. He was acquitted on the basis that filming a person without consent was not an offence. The Court held that the absence from domestic law of a remedy which would have enabled the applicant to obtain effective protection against the violation of her personal integrity amounted to a breach of art.8.

It was also said, in *Douglas v Hello! Ltd* (2005), that the Court has "recognised an obligation on Member States to protect one individual from unjustified invasion of private life by another" (the context being the activities of paparazzi).

9. RIGHT TO RESPECT FOR FREEDOM OF THOUGHT, CONSCIENCE AND RELIGION (ARTICLE 9)

INTRODUCTION

9–01 The scheme of art.9 is very similar to that of art.8. Article 9.1 states the right and art.9.2 states the basis on which that right may be limited. The full text is as follows:

> 1. Everyone has the right to freedom of thought, conscience and religion; this right includes freedom to change his religion or belief and freedom, either alone or in community with others and in public or private, to manifest his religion or belief, in worship, teaching, practice and observance.

> 2. Freedom to manifest one's religion or beliefs shall be subject only to such limitations as are prescribed by law and are necessary in a democratic society in the interests of public safety, for the protection of public order, health or morals, or for the protection of the rights and freedoms of others.

It should be noted at the outset that the right belongs to individuals, not to companies, because a company lacks the capacity to have a conscience or religious belief (*Company X v Switzerland* (1981)). It should also be noted that in *Manoussakis v Greece* (1997) the Court said that the right to freedom of religion as guaranteed under the Convention excludes any discretion on the part of the state to determine whether religious beliefs or the means used to express such beliefs are legitimate.

THOUGHT, CONSCIENCE AND RELIGION

9–02 There are three concepts involved in this right and they are not synonymous:
- thought;
- conscience; and
- religion.

The extent to which thought, conscience and religion overlap has not really been explored in the case law. It is clear, both from the text of the article and from *Kokkinakis v Greece* (1993) (in which the Court said that as well as being vital for believers, the right is also a "precious asset for atheists, agnostics, sceptics and the unconcerned") that thought and conscience are not merely subheadings of religion. In the case law of the Commission and the Court (which is very limited) the main focus has, however, been on religion (because that has been the heading under which most applicants have gone to the Court).

TEACHING

The Court confirmed in *Kokkinakis* that teaching includes the right to **9–03** evangelise and the decision in *Redmond-Bate v DPP* (2000) was consistent with that (albeit reached by reference to art.10). In that case, the appellant was preaching outside a cathedral and had drawn a crowd of about 100, some of whom were heckling. A police officer required her to stop preaching and, when she refused, arrested her and charged her with wilful obstruction of a police officer. It was held that in this case art.9 added nothing to the guarantees in art.10, upon the basis of which the case should be determined. The arrest had violated the appellant's art.10 right to freedom of expression and therefore had no lawful basis.

"PRACTICE"

In *Hasan v Bulgaria* (2002), the Strasbourg Court held that participation in **9–04** the life of the religious community is a manifestation of one's religion, protected by art.9. The Court further found that where the organisation of the religious community is at issue art.9 should be interpreted in the light of art.11, which safeguards associative life against unjustified state interference. Seen in this perspective, the believer's right to freedom of religion encompasses the expectation that the community will be allowed to function peacefully, free from arbitrary state intervention. Indeed, the Court considered, the autonomous existence of religious communities is indispensable for pluralism in a democratic society and is thus an issue at the very heart of the protection afforded by art.9. In *Hasan*, interference by the state in decisions about who should be appointed as the leader of a Muslim community was held to be a breach of art.9.

The interference in *Perry v Latvia* (2008) was less direct but was, nonetheless, interference. The residence permit of a foreign missionary, who served as the pastor of a parish, was replaced with one that did not allow him to organise public activities of a religious nature. Article 9 was held to be engaged.

Like worship, teaching and observance, "practice" is contemplated only in relation to religion. In *Pretty v United Kingdom* (2002), the Court said that not all opinions or convictions constitute beliefs in the sense protected by art.9. In that case, the Court said that the applicant's claims did not involve a form of manifestation of a religion or belief, through worship, teaching, practice or observance. Accordingly, although she asserted that she "believed in" the notion of assisted suicide, there was no breach.

In *Arrowsmith v United Kingdom* (1978), the applicant argued that her **9–05** distribution of pacifist leaflets to soldiers (in respect of which she was convicted) was motivated by her pacifist beliefs and hence protected by art.9. The Commission accepted that pacifism falls within the ambit of the right to freedom of thought, conscience and religion but held that the term "practice" in art.9.1 does not cover absolutely every act that is motivated or influenced by a religion or a belief. In *Larissis v Greece* (1998) the Court recalled this principle in holding that there had been no breach of art.9 where members of the Pentecostal Church had been convicted of proselytism (in some circumstances an offence under Greek law) where those whom they sought to convert were their subordinates in the Greek air force and testified that they had felt under pressure because of the difference in rank. In the same case, however, the Court held that there was a breach in respect of convictions for attempting to convert civilians who did not feel themselves under any pressure. This approach applied a distinction drawn in *Kokkinakis*. In that case, the Court said that bearing Christian witness and improper proselytism are not the same thing. The former, it said, corresponds to true evangelism, which a report drawn up in 1956 under the auspices of the World Council of Churches ("WCC") described as an essential mission and a responsibility of every Christian and every Church. The latter, the Court said, represents a corruption or deformation of it. Improper proselytism, according to the WCC report, may take the form of activities offering material or social advantages with a view to gaining new members for a Church or exerting improper pressure on people in distress or in need; it may even entail the use of violence or brainwashing. These practices, the Court said, are not compatible with respect for the freedom of thought, conscience and religion of others.

The Commission applied a similar approach in cases in which applicants had attempted, on the basis of their religious beliefs, to withhold tax since that tax went into a general fund, some of which was used to purchase armaments. The Commission said (in *H; B v United Kingdom* (1986)) that art.9

> "primarily protects the sphere of personal beliefs and religious creeds, i.e. the area which is sometimes called the forum internum. In addition, it protects acts which are intimately linked to these attitudes, such as acts of worship or devotion which are aspects of the practice of a religion or belief in a generally recognised form. However, in protecting this personal sphere, Article 9 of the Convention does not always guarantee the right to behave in the public sphere in a way which is dictated by such a belief: for instance by refusing to pay certain taxes because part of the revenue so raised may be applied for military expenditure ... The obligation to pay taxes is a general one which has no specific conscientious implications in itself".

ARTICLE 9 AS AN ALTERNATIVE TO OTHER ARTICLES

Some applicants have noted that art.9.2 permits the state to interfere with **9–06** the manifestation of religion or beliefs but that there is in the Convention no basis on which the state can interfere with freedom of thought or conscience. This has meant that art.9 becomes an attractive alternative to other articles, such as art.8, which permit more wide-ranging state interference. If an applicant can characterise an issue as relating to the realm of thought or conscience rather than simply to their private or family life (for example) the fact that the state might, in response to a pressing social need, have been acting lawfully and proportionately in pursuit of an art.8.2 objective becomes irrelevant. The Court has, however, consistently declined to accept such lines of argument. In *Hoffman v Austria* (1993) the applicant was unsuccessful in invoking art.9 in relation to the custody of children where the parents had different religious beliefs; the Court dealt with the issue under art.8. In *Young, James and Webster v United Kingdom* (1981) issues relating to the refusal, out of conviction, of the applicants to join a trade union were addressed by the Court under art.11, not art.9.

10. RIGHT TO FREEDOM OF EXPRESSION
(ARTICLE 10)

INTRODUCTION

10–01 Article 10 provides:

> 1. Everyone has the right to freedom of expression. This right shall include freedom to hold opinions and to receive and impart information and ideas without interference by public authority and regardless of frontiers. This Article shall not prevent States from requiring the licensing of broadcasting, television or cinema enterprises.
>
> 2. The exercise of these freedoms, since it carries with it duties and responsibilities, may be subject to such formalities, conditions, restrictions or penalties as are prescribed by law and are necessary in a democratic society, in the interests of national security, territorial integrity or public safety, for the prevention of disorder or crime, for the protection of health or morals, for the protection of the reputation or rights of others, for preventing the disclosure of information received in confidence, or for maintaining the authority and impartiality of the judiciary.

Like other articles, art.10 begins by stating the right and then goes on to state the qualifications and restrictions which apply to it. It will be seen that the structure of art.10.2 bears a marked similarity to that of art.8.2, in that it adopts the same formula of "prescribed by law", "necessary" and legitimate objectives. Many of the objectives are the same as those which apply to art.8 but there are certain additional ones. There is also a preamble which explains that the exercise of the freedom carries with it duties and responsibilities. In *Bergens Tidende v Norway* (2000) the Court pointed out that by reason of the "duties and responsibilities" inherent in the exercise of freedom of expression, the safeguard afforded by art.10 to journalists in relation to reporting on issues of general interest is subject to the proviso that they must act in good faith in order to provide accurate and reliable information in accordance with the ethics of journalism.

THE AMBIT OF THE RIGHT

10–02 The right to freedom of expression is a right which is guaranteed to all. It was made clear in *Casado Coca v Spain* (1994) that "no distinction is made in it according to whether the type of aim is profit making or not". This principle enabled the applicant in that case to complain (albeit ultimately unsuccessfully) that it was a breach of art.10 for him as a lawyer to be penalised for advertising. Nor is the right restricted to the expression of ideas that are inoffensive (*Redmond-Bate v DPP* (2000)) or not shocking (*Open Door and Dublin Well Woman v Ireland* (1992)).

Paragraph 1 makes it clear that the right includes freedom to hold opinions and to receive and impart information and ideas. In terms of the definition, it has a very wide ambit. Also in *Casado Coca*, the Court said that art.10

"does not apply solely to certain types of information or ideas or forms of expression, in particular those of a political nature; it also encompasses artistic expression, information of a commercial nature ... and even light music and commercials transmitted by cable".

The article has been held applicable not only to advertisements (*Casado Coca* (1994)) but also to investigative journalism (*Sunday Times v United Kingdom* (1979–1980)) and to artistic works. In *Muller v Switzerland* (1988), the Court explained that art.10 does not distinguish between the various forms of expression. Indeed, art.10 applies even where the work in question might be regarded as devoid of any real artistic merit. In *Muller*, the Swiss appellate court rejected evidence that the paintings at issue had any artistic merit, observing that in them "sexual activity is crudely and vulgarly portrayed for its own sake and not as a consequence of any idea informing the work".

This is not to say that considerations of morality have no relevance to art.10; merely that the proper approach is to address those considerations under the heading of art.10.2, which sets out the cases in which there may be interference with the right to freedom of expression.

The concept of freedom of expression, then, is a wide one but it is not unlimited. The words "freedom of expression" have to be given their ordinary meaning in their context and that context deals with opinions, information and ideas. In *Stevens v UK* (1986) the Commission held that it does not include expressing oneself sexually by having intercourse; the application in that case was by a serving prisoner who complained that being prevented from having sexual relations was a breach of art.10. In *Kosiek v FRG* (1986) the applicants were unsuccessful in their attempt to bring the attachment of conditions to their employment as teachers within art.10. On the facts, what the complaint was really about was rights of access to public employment.

INTERFERENCE WITH THE RIGHT

In the range of cases to which the right to freedom of expression does **10–03** properly apply, the interferences with which the Court has typically had to deal have frequently involved interdicts and convictions for obscenity and contempt of court. There is no doubt that all of these things are interferences. The Court explained in *Handyside v United Kingdom* (1979–1980) and *Sunday Times v United Kingdom* (1979–1980) that an interference entails a violation of art.10 if it does not fall within one of the exceptions provided for in art.10.2. Where this stage is reached, the Court therefore has to examine in turn whether the interference "prescribed by law", whether it had an aim or aims that is or are legitimate under art.10.2 and whether it was "necessary in a democratic society" for that aim or aims.

PRESCRIBED BY LAW AND LEGITIMATE AIMS

10–04 The expression "prescribed by law" is by now a familiar one that does not require elaboration; though it is worth noting that in *Casado Coca* (1994) the Statute of the Spanish Bar was a sufficient basis for a finding that this criterion was satisfied. Similarly, the acceptable aims that art.10.2 articulates are, for the most part, familiar. The key question under art.10 has usually been whether the necessity of the interference has been made out.

NECESSITY

Politics

10–05 It is well recognised that states have a wide margin of appreciation in this matter but it has also to be recognised that this margin is appreciably narrowed where the purpose of the expression involved is political rather than commercial or artistic. In *Castells v Spain* (1992) the applicant had been convicted of the offence of insulting the government. He was an elected member of the Spanish legislature and he had published an article in which he alleged inactivity on the part of the authorities, in particular the police, in face of terrorist murders in the Basque country and even collusion between the police and the guilty parties. In convicting him, the national court stressed that the state could be threatened by attempts to discredit democratic institutions. In the context of a considerable terrorist campaign the Court was willing to accept that the proceedings instituted against the applicant were brought for the prevention of disorder within the meaning of art.10.2.

The Court noted that the applicant had made his criticism in a periodical and pointed out that the "pre-eminent role of the press in a State governed by the rule of law" must not be forgotten. Although it must not overstep various bounds set for the prevention of disorder and the protection of the reputation of others, it is, the Court said, nevertheless incumbent on it to impart information and ideas on political questions and on other matters of public interest. Freedom of the press affords the public one of the best means of discovering and forming an opinion of the ideas and attitudes of their political leaders. The Court said that free political debate is at the very core of the concept of a democratic society, though it added that the freedom of political debate is not absolute in nature. In an important passage, it went on to say:

> "The limits of permissible criticism are wider with regard to the Government than in relation to a private citizen, or even a politician. In a democratic system the actions or omissions of the Government must be subject to the close scrutiny not only of the legislative and judicial authorities but also of the press and public opinion. Furthermore, the dominant position which the Government occupies makes it necessary for it to display restraint in resorting to criminal proceedings, particularly where other means are available for replying to the unjustified attacks and criticisms of its adversaries or the media."

Similarly, the Court has taken an unsympathetic view to attempts to restrain political protest. In *Steel v United Kingdom* (1999) the third, fourth and fifth applicants had been engaged in a peaceful protest outside the "Fighter Helicopter II" conference in London, a marketing event, at which combat helicopters were being sold. They were all arrested and presented to court from custody. On that occasion, the case was adjourned and, when it next called, the prosecution offered no evidence, so the case was dismissed. The Court held that there had been a breach of art.10. The applicants had been committing no offence and their arrest was, therefore, an interference with the exercise of their right to freedom of expression which was disproportionate to the prevention of disorder and protection of the rights of others as authorised by the Convention.

Similar considerations arose in *R (Laporte) v Chief Constable of Gloucestershire Constabulary* (2007), in which the House of Lords held that there had been an unlawful interference with the claimant's rights under arts 10 and 11. She had been travelling to a protest demonstration in Gloucestershire but the police intercepted the coaches carrying demonstrators, turned them back and escorted them back to London, so that they were prevented from attending the demonstration at all.

The press

There is also a tendency on the part of the Court to be unsympathetic to attempts to restrain press freedom. There were elements of this in *Castells* but it appears still more clearly in cases which have been pursued in Strasbourg by newspapers or journalists themselves. The best known example of this is the *Sunday Times* case in which the Court held (by a narrow margin of 9:7) that an injunction obtained by the Attorney General restraining publication of an article was not necessary in that it did not meet a pressing social need. The context was that there was ongoing litigation about the drug thalidomide, which had been taken by a number of pregnant women and which had caused deformities in their children. The article was part of a newspaper campaign to secure a better settlement for the claimants and was to address the history of the testing, manufacture and marketing of

10–06

the drug. The injunction proceeded on the basis that the article would constitute a contempt of court.

The Court said art.10 is of particular importance where the press is concerned and that whilst the mass media must not overstep the bounds imposed in the interests of the proper administration of justice, it is incumbent on them to impart information and ideas concerning matters that come before the courts. "Not only do the media have the task of imparting such information and ideas", said the Court, "the public also has a right to receive them". In the particular case, the families of the victims had a vital interest in knowing the underlying facts and they could be deprived of that information "only if it appeared absolutely certain that its diffusion would have presented a threat to the authority of the judiciary."

A similar determination to protect the freedom of the press appeared in *Barthold v FRG* (1985). In that case a vet who had been campaigning for a round-the-clock veterinary emergency service was party to a newspaper article that described how the life of a cat had been saved only because he provided such a service. This got him into difficulties with his professional body and resulted ultimately in him being the subject of an order restraining him from publishing certain types of material.

10–07 The Court found a breach of art.10, noting that the article had pursued the specific object of informing the public about a situation at a time when the enactment of new legislation on veterinary surgeons was under consideration. The Court said that freedom of expression constitutes one of the essential foundations of a democratic society and one of the basic conditions for its progress and for the development of every man and woman. The necessity for restricting that freedom for one of the purposes listed in art.10.2 must be convincingly established.

When considered from this viewpoint, the interference complained of went further than the requirements of the legitimate aim pursued. The domestic law presumed that a professional who wrote an article intended to act for the purposes of commercial competition as long as that intent has not been entirely over-ridden by other motives; but the Court considered that a criterion as strict as this in approaching the matter of advertising and publicity in the liberal professions is not consonant with freedom of expression. Its application risks discouraging members of the liberal professions from contributing to public debate on topics affecting the life of the community if ever there is the slightest likelihood of their utterances being treated as entailing, to some degree, an advertising effect. By the same token, application of a criterion such as this is liable to hamper the press in the performance of its task of purveyor of information and public watchdog.

By contrast, we should note *Ahmed v United Kingdom* (2000), which concerned restrictions on the political activities of some relatively senior local government employees. The Court held that the interferences that resulted from the application of the restrictions to the applicants pursued the legitimate aim of protecting the rights of others, council members and the electorate alike, to effective political democracy at the local level. The intention behind the regulations was to underpin the long tradition of political neutrality that local government officers owed to elected council members and to ensure that the effectiveness of local political democracy was not diminished through the corrosion of the neutrality of certain categories of officers characterised by the sensitivity of their functions. The restrictions were, in part, a reaction to specific instances of abuse of power by certain local government officers and that there was increased potential for more widespread abuse in the light of a trend towards confrontational politics in local government affairs. The restrictions were a valid response to that problem and they only applied to carefully defined categories of senior officers distinguished by the nature of the activities they performed and in respect of which political impartiality was a paramount consideration. The right to join a political party was not affected but only the freedom of senior officers to make public pronouncements that appeared to be of a party political nature.

Other issues

States have been much more successful where the expression of political **10–08** views has not been the matter for consideration. In *Handyside* (1979–1980) the Court held that the conviction on obscenity charges of a man who published a book aimed at children which included highly explicit and controversial advice on sex was a proportionate and justifiable response to a threat to morality. The applicant in *Muller*, with his distasteful paintings, was unsuccessful on the same ground.

In *Otto-Preminger-Institut v Austria* (1994) and in *Wingrove v United Kingdom* (1996) the Court found no breach where states had penalised the makers of films that were likely to be seriously offensive to Christians and recalled that the exercise of freedom of expression carries with it duties and responsibilities. Amongst them, it said, in the context of religious beliefs, may legitimately be included a duty to avoid as far as possible an expression that is, in regard to objects of veneration, gratuitously offensive to others and profanatory. In *Wingrove*, one judge added a separate concurring opinion in which he pointed out that the rights of the adherents of other religions would have received similar protection.

This is not, however, to say that states will always be successful where the issue relates to a matter other than politics. In *Open Door and Dublin Well Woman v Ireland* (1992) the applicants were companies and individuals who were engaged in counselling pregnant women. An injunction had been obtained against them to restrain them from providing information about abortion facilities outside the jurisdiction of Ireland (where abortion could not lawfully be carried out).

The Court found it appropriate to recall that freedom of expression is applicable to "information" or "ideas" that offend, shock or disturb the state or any sector of the population. Such are the demands of that pluralism, tolerance and broadmindedness without which there is no "democratic society".

The injunction had been of an absolute nature. It imposed a "perpetual" restraint on the provision of information to pregnant women concerning abortion facilities abroad, regardless of age or state of health or their reasons for seeking counselling on the termination of pregnancy. On that ground alone the restriction appeared to the Court to be over-broad and disproportionate.

Moreover, information concerning abortion facilities abroad could be obtained from other sources in Ireland such as magazines and telephone directories or by persons with contacts in Great Britain. Accordingly, information that the injunction sought to restrict was already available elsewhere.

The Court concluded that the restraint imposed on the applicants from receiving or imparting information was disproportionate to the aims pursued and held that there had been a breach of art.10.

11. RIGHT TO FREEDOM OF ASSEMBLY
(ARTICLE 11)

INTRODUCTION

Article 11 provides: **11–01**

1. Everyone has the right to freedom of peaceful assembly and to freedom of association with others, including the right to form and to join trade unions for the protection of his interests.

2. No restrictions shall be placed on the exercise of these rights other than such as are prescribed by law and are necessary in a democratic society in the interests of national security or public safety, for the prevention of disorder or crime, for the protection of health or morals or for the protection of the rights and freedoms of others. This article shall not prevent the imposition of lawful restrictions on the exercise of these rights by members of the armed forces, of the police or of the administration of the State.

This guarantees two rights: freedom of assembly; and freedom of association.

FREEDOM OF ASSEMBLY

Freedom of assembly has not been considered in any great detail by the **11–02** Strasbourg Court and Commission; but the meaning of the word "assembly" is straightforward enough and some illumination can be gained from the cases, which tend to concern public demonstrations (for example, *Plattform "Arzte Fur Das Leben" v Austria* (1991); *Christians against Racism and Facism v United Kingdom* (1980)). It is clear that the right is applicable both to public and private assembly (*Rassemblement Jurassien Unité v Switzerland* (1979)). The right is, however, to peaceful assembly and cannot be claimed by those having violent intentions (*G v Federal Republic of Germany* (1989)).

FREEDOM OF ASSOCIATION

Freedom of association is generally regarded as the right to join with others **11–03** to achieve a particular end. It includes the right to form and join a political party (*United Communist Party of Turkey v Turkey* (1998)) and it also includes the right to form and join trade unions. So far as trade unions are concerned, however, the Court has made it clear that art.11 does not guarantee any particular treatment of trade unions, or their members, by the state, such as the right to be consulted by it (*National Union of Belgian Police Case* (1979–1980)). Moreover, in *Young, James and Webster v United Kingdom* (1981), the Court pointed out that the notion of a freedom implies some measure of freedom of choice as to its exercise. It therefore reasoned that to construe art.11 as permitting compulsion in the field of trade union membership would strike at the very substance of the freedom it is designed to guarantee (in that case, the applicants had been sacked for refusing to join a union where the industry was subject to a "closed shop" agreement).

INTERFERENCES

11–04 Interferences with the rights of freedom of assembly and of association have taken several forms. The mere application of a prior authorisation procedure does not amount on its own to an interference (*Rassemblement Jurassien Unité v Switzerland*) but the banning or imposing of conditions upon an assembly or association with lawful intent is very likely to do so. In such a case, the issues will be, as in relation to other articles, whether the three heads of art.11.2 are satisfied:

- Is the interference prescribed by law?
- Does the interference pursue one of the specified, legitimate objectives?
- Is the interference necessary (that is, does it address a pressing social need and is it proportionate)?

NECESSITY

11–05 As so often, the issues before the Court have related principally to the question of necessity and, in particular, proportionality. The Court has made a point of saying that it considers each art.11 case on its own facts and extrapolation from decided cases is therefore difficult and unwise. However, the Commission has held that the banning of trade unions at a government intelligence establishment was proportionate to the need to maintain national security (*Council of Civil Service Unions v United Kingdom* (1987)). In *Vogt v Germany* (1996), on the other hand, the Court held that the dismissal of a state-employed school teacher because she refused to dissociate herself from a left wing political party was excessive. In particular, the Court considered that the concept of the "administration of the state" had to be understood quite narrowly. In *United Communist Party of Turkey* (1998), the Court said that the exceptions set out in art.11.2 have to be construed particularly strictly where political parties are concerned.

POSITIVE OBLIGATION

There is a clear positive obligation inherent in art.11. In *Plattform "Arzte* **11–06**
Fur Das Leben" (1991) an association of doctors who were campaigning
against abortion held two demonstrations that were disrupted by counter-
demonstrators despite the presence of a large contingent of police. The
applicants complained that they had not had sufficient police protection
during the demonstrations and that there had been a violation of arts 9, 10
and 11 of the Convention. The Court observed that a demonstration may
annoy or give offence to persons opposed to the ideas or claims that it is
seeking to promote but that the participants must nevertheless be able to
hold the demonstration without having to fear that they will be subjected
to physical violence by their opponents; such a fear would be liable to deter
associations or other groups supporting common ideas or interests from
openly expressing their opinions on highly controversial issues affecting
the community. In a democracy the right to counter-demonstrate cannot
extend to inhibiting the exercise of the right to demonstrate. Genuine,
effective freedom of peaceful assembly cannot, therefore, be reduced to a
mere duty on the part of the state not to interfere: a purely negative
conception would not be compatible with the object and purpose of art.11.
Like art.8, art.11 sometimes requires positive measures to be taken.

Having thus established the existence of a positive obligation, the Court
considered its content. The Court explained that, while it is the duty of
contracting states to take reasonable and appropriate measures to enable
lawful demonstrations to proceed peacefully, they cannot guarantee this
absolutely and they have a wide discretion in the choice of the means to be
used. In this area the obligation they enter into under art.11 of the
Convention is an obligation as to measures to be taken and not as to results
to be achieved. In the instant case, the Court considered that the Austrian
authorities did not fail to take reasonable and appropriate measures, so that
the positive obligation was satisfied.

12. RIGHT TO PEACEFUL ENJOYMENT OF POSSESSIONS (PROTOCOL 1 ARTICLE 1)

INTRODUCTION

12–01 Article 1 of Protocol 1 provides:

> Every natural or legal person is entitled to the peaceful enjoyment of his possessions. No one shall be deprived of his possessions except in the public interest and subject to the conditions provided for by law and by the general principles of international law.
>
> The preceding provisions shall not, however, in any way impair the right of a State to enforce such laws as it deems necessary to control the use of property in accordance with the general interest or to secure the payment of taxes or other contributions or penalties.

POSSESSIONS

12–02 It will be seen that the Convention uses the word "possessions" primarily, not the word "property". "Possessions" is an autonomous concept, not limited to property rights as recognised by domestic law. It will be understood that "property" is a complex concept even in a single legal system. It is far too complex to form the basis of a rule applicable to over 40 systems.

"Possessions" is wider than most understandings of "property". In *Gasus Dosier und Fördertechnik GmbH v the Netherlands* (1995) the Court said that it

> "is certainly not limited to ownership of physical goods: certain other rights and interests constituting assets can also be regarded as 'property rights', and thus as 'possessions', for the purposes of this provision".

So in that case the right was held to apply to the seller's interest in property sold under retention of title, delivered but not paid for and seized by the tax authorities in respect of the purchaser's tax debts. In other cases, it has been held to apply to such disparate "assets" as land occupied for a century but without a formal title (*Matos e Silva v Portugal* (1996)), a licence to serve alcohol in a restaurant (*Tre Traktorer v Sweden* (1989)) and certain succession rights (*Inze v Austria* (1987)).

THE THREE RULES

Introduction

In *Sporrong and Lönroth v Sweden* (1982) the Court explained the way in   **12–03** which the article works and the way in which it will be approached by the Court. The article, the Court said, comprises three distinct rules:

> "The first rule, which is of a general nature, enounces the principle of peaceful enjoyment of property; it is set out in the first sentence of the first paragraph. The second rule covers deprivation of possessions and subjects it to certain conditions; it appears in the second sentence of the same paragraph. The third rule recognises that the States are entitled, amongst other things, to control the use of property in accordance with the general interest, by enforcing such laws as they deem necessary for the purpose; it is contained in the second paragraph."

This is not, at first, especially easy to follow; but the Court went on to say that it "must determine, before considering whether the first rule was complied with, whether the last two are applicable". We therefore look first at the second rule, which deals with deprivation of property.

Deprivation of property

For the second rule to apply, there has to have been a taking or   **12–04** expropriation of property. This is not, however, simply a question of whether there has been an expropriation as a matter of law. In *Sporrong and Lönroth* the facts were that the Government had granted the Stockholm City Council a "zonal expropriation permit" covering 164 properties, including that owned by the first applicant. As matters finally stood, the city council had 23 years within which to expropriate the property. There was an associated prohibition on construction work which subsisted for 25 years. Similar orders affected the second applicant, though for shorter periods of time. The existence of these orders made it exceptionally difficult for the applicants to sell or let their property or to borrow on its security.

The Court noted that the authorities did not proceed to an expropriation of the applicants' properties in the sense that they were not formally deprived of their possessions at any time. This, however, was not the end of the matter. In the absence of a formal expropriation transfer of ownership, the Court considered that it had to look behind the appearances and investigate the realities of the situation. It recalled that the Convention is intended to guarantee rights that are practical and effective and so it had to be ascertained whether that situation amounted to a de facto expropriation, as was argued by the applicants. On the particular facts, the Court held that, although the right in question lost some of its substance, it did not disappear. The effects of the measures involved were not such that they could be assimilated to a deprivation of possessions. There was therefore no room for the application of the second sentence of the first paragraph in the case; but the Court signalled clearly that there could be cases in which something short of legal deprivation of property might amount to deprivation for the purposes of the Convention. That was precisely what happened in *Papamichalopoulos v Greece* (1993) in which legislation transferred the use of land from the applicants to the Navy Fund, leaving the applicants with a bare and, in practice, utterly unmarketable title. In that case, the Court held that the second rule applied.

Control of use

12–05 In *Sporrong*, the Court, having held that the second rule did not apply, went on to consider the third. That relates to controls on the use of property. The Court held that the prohibitions on construction clearly amounted to a control of the use of the property but that the expropriation permits were not intended to limit or control such use. The third rule therefore applied to the prohibitions on construction.

Air Canada v United Kingdom (1995), on the other hand, was a case in which there was held to have been a control of use. The facts were that on a number of occasions between 1983 and 1987 incidents of drug smuggling gave rise to concern over the adequacy of the applicant company's security procedures at Heathrow airport, London. Customs and Excise wrote expressing concern about this and the applicants promised to improve their security. On December 15, 1986 Customs and Excise wrote to all airline operators at Heathrow and Gatwick warning them that consideration would be given to the seizure and forfeiture of aircraft where drug smuggling occurred. On April 26, 1987 an aircraft owned and operated by the applicants and worth over £60 million, landed at Heathrow where it discharged a container that was found to contain 331 kilograms of cannabis resin valued at about £800,000. The documentation for the container was incomplete and false. On May 1, 1987, at a time when passengers were waiting to board the aircraft, Customs officers seized it as liable to forfeiture. On the same day the Commissioners of Customs and Excise delivered the aircraft back to the applicant company on payment of a penalty of £50,000. The applicants complained to the Commission that the seizure of its aircraft and its subsequent return on conditions violated art.1 of Protocol No.1. The Government contended that this was not a case involving a deprivation of property since no transfer of ownership of the applicant's aircraft had taken place. Rather, the seizure and demand for payment were to be seen as part of the system for the control of the use of an aircraft which had been employed for the import of prohibited drugs. The Court held that the Government's analysis was correct and that the seizure of the aircraft amounted to a temporary restriction on its use and did not involve a transfer of ownership. It therefore had to be decided whether the interference with the applicant's property rights was in conformity with the State's right under the second paragraph of art.1 of Protocol No. 1 "to enforce such laws as it deems necessary to control the use of property in accordance with the general interest". According to the Court, that paragraph had to be construed in the light of the principle laid down in the Article's first sentence, so that it must achieve a "fair balance" between the demands of the general interest of the community and the requirements of the protection of the individual's fundamental rights. There must be a reasonable relationship of proportionality between the means employed and the aim pursued. While the width of the powers of forfeiture conferred on the Commissioners of Customs and Excise was striking, the seizure of the applicant's aircraft and its release subject to payment were undoubtedly exceptional measures which were resorted to in order to bring about an improvement in the company's security procedures. The incident was the latest in a long series of alleged security lapses which had been brought to the applicants' attention. There could be no doubt that the measures taken conformed to the general interest in combating international drug trafficking. Taking into account the large quantity of cannabis that was found and the value of the aircraft that had been seized, the Court did not consider the requirement to pay £50,000 to be disproportionate to the aim pursued, namely the prevention of the importation of prohibited drugs into the UK.

Peaceful enjoyment of possessions
As to prohibitions on construction in *Sporrong*, the question for the Court **12–06** was whether a fair balance was struck between the demands of the general interest of the community and the requirements of the protection of the individual's fundamental rights. This is proportionality otherwise expressed. In the particular case, the Court held that the applicable legal regime was so inflexible and applied for such a long time as to upset that balance. It therefore found a breach of the article and did not analyse the matter further; though it had commented, by way of preamble to its judgement, that the expropriation permits affected the very substance of ownership and rendered the applicants' right of property precarious and defeasible. That being so, the Court considered that there was an interference with the applicants' right of property. It seems likely that, had it required to consider the matter, the Court would have found the first rule applicable.

CONDITIONS PROVIDED FOR BY LAW

Whichever of the rules contemplated by the article applies, an interference **12–07** with the peaceful enjoyment of possessions must be subject to conditions provided for by law (equivalent to "prescribed by law" in other articles), in the public interest and proportionate.

PUBLIC INTEREST

The public interest criterion was in the mind of the Court in *Raimondo v* **12–08** *Italy* (1994). In that case, the applicant was prosecuted, and ultimately acquitted, on charges relating to his alleged membership of a mafia-type organisation. In connection with the prosecution, the Italian court had ordered preventive seizure of certain land, buildings and vehicles. It subsequently ordered the confiscation of some of those assets on the ground that it had not been proved that they had been lawfully acquired. Following the applicant's acquittal the return of the confiscated property was ordered. There was, however, delay of over four years in the return of some of the property. The applicant complained that the confiscation had breached art.1 of Protocol 1 in itself and in that the property had not been adequately supervised and had suffered damage. The Court held that the seizure was

> "clearly a provisional measure intended to ensure that property which appears to be the fruit of unlawful activities carried out to the detriment of the community can subsequently be confiscated if necessary. The measure as such was therefore justified by the general interest and, in view of the extremely dangerous economic power of an 'organisation' like the Mafia, it cannot be said that taking it at this stage of the proceedings was disproportionate to the aim pursued".

As to the damage, the Court held that this was an inevitable consequence of any seizure or confiscation. It was not clear that the damage sustained exceeded that which was inevitable. However, the Court found it hard to see why there had been such a long delay in returning property to the applicant and in that respect (but only in that respect) there was a breach of art.1 of Protocol 1.

PROPORTIONALITY

12–09 *Raimondo* (1994) was, of course, a somewhat extreme case. The Council of Europe has taken a lead in the agreement of treaties to deal with organised crime and its proceeds and a robust approach to any case with that element alleged was to be expected. *Raimondo* should be seen against the background of *AGOSI v United Kingdom* (1987), in which the Court pointed out that the second paragraph of art.1 of Protocol 1 recognises the right of a State "to enforce such laws as it deems necessary to control the use of property ... in accordance with the general interest". The Court stressed that there must be proportionality in this and said that the striking of a fair balance depends on many factors and the behaviour of the owner of the property, including the degree of fault or care which he has displayed, is one element of the entirety of circumstances which should be taken into account. The Court also said that there is a substantial margin of appreciation involved in art.1 of Protocol 1.

13. OTHER RIGHTS

INTRODUCTION

In the foregoing chapters, we have looked at the Convention rights that **13–01** have generated most case law. The remaining Convention rights, whilst far from unimportant, are dealt with in this chapter in rather less detail than the other rights.

ARTICLE 4

Introduction
Article 4 is the prohibition on slavery and forced labour. It provides: **13–02**

1. No one shall be held in slavery or servitude. No one shall be required to perform forced or compulsory labour.

2. For the purpose of this Article the term "forced or compulsory labour" shall not include:

(a) any work required to be done in the ordinary course of detention imposed according to the provisions of Article 5 of this Convention or during conditional release from such detention;
(b) any service of a military character or, in case of conscientious objectors in countries where they are recognised, service exacted instead of compulsory military service;
(c) any service exacted in case of an emergency or calamity threatening the life or well-being of the community;
(d) any work or service which forms part of normal civic obligations.

Slavery
There are two rights here. The first is the right not to be held in slavery or **13–03** servitude. No case exists in which the Court or Commission have taken the view that a state party to ECHR was in breach of this and the concept of slavery has not even been considered in any case. "Servitude" was considered briefly in *Van Droogenbroeck v Belgium* (1982) and found not to be relevant to the case of a convicted prisoner who was required to undertake work in the course of his sentence.

Forced labour
The second right, which is the right not to be required to perform forced or **13–04** compulsory labour, was considered in *Van der Mussele v Belgium* (1983).

The applicant was a Belgian avocat (lawyer) who had been required, as part of his professional obligations, to act for a person who was indigent and who received no remuneration for so doing. He complained that the fact that he had not been entitled to any remuneration or reimbursement of his expenses gave rise both to "forced or compulsory labour". The case was, in short, one which was not calculated to engage the sympathies of a Court composed of judges who had probably all had to meet similar professional obligations during their careers. However, in the course of holding that there had not been any breach of art.4, the Court did offer some explanation of the concept of forced and compulsory labour and the case is useful because of that.

The Court said that art.4 is based, to a large extent, on an earlier treaty of the International Labour Organisation, namely Convention No.29 concerning forced or compulsory labour. The main aim of that Convention was originally to prevent the exploitation of labour in colonies, which were still numerous at that time and under it, the term "forced or compulsory labour" meant

> "all work or service which is exacted from any person under the menace of any penalty and for which the said person has not offered himself voluntarily".

This definition provides a starting point for interpretation of art.4 of ECHR but sight should not be lost of the fact that ECHR is a living instrument to be read "in the light of the notions currently prevailing in democratic States".

According to the Court, in the phrase "forced or compulsory" labour the adjective "forced" connotes physical or mental constraint. The second adjective, "compulsory" does not refer to absolutely any form of legal compulsion or obligation. What there has to be is work exacted under the menace of a penalty and also performed against the will of the person concerned, that is, work for which he had not offered himself voluntarily. The Court also considered that the work required would have to be disproportionately onerous.

ARTICLE 12

13–05 Article 12 simply provides:

> "Men and women of marriageable age have the right to marry and to found a family, according to the national laws governing the exercise of this right."

The Court explained in *Rees v UK* (1986) that the article is mainly concerned to protect marriage as the basis of the family; and whilst it has been willing to give "family" quite a wide interpretation in art.8, the Court has not shown itself willing to extend art.12 beyond marriage as traditionally recognised. This, as the Court pointed out in *Johnston v Ireland*, reflects the original intention of the contracting states. The article also offers some illumination of the concept of the Convention as a "living instrument". In *Cossey v UK* (1990), notwithstanding the significant changes in social attitudes to cohabitation, homosexual and transsexual relationships since the entry into force of the Convention, the Court attached some importance to the fact that there was no evidence that there had been any abandonment by contracting states of the traditional concept of marriage. In that case, and in *Rees* before it, the Court refused to hold that art.12 entitled a postoperative transsexual to marry in their new gender. The reasoning was that the article gives the right to marry to "men and women" and that it was biologically heterosexual unions that the contracting states had in mind. In *Schalk and Kopf v Austria* (2011), the Court held, on an application by two men who wished to marry each other, that although art.12 did not expressly provide that a man could only marry a woman it was clear that, given the historical context in which the Convention was adopted and the traditional understanding of marriage, that was what art.12 meant. The Court went on to observe that although the Convention was a living instrument and the institution of marriage had undergone significant change since the Convention was drafted, there was no clear European consensus on same-sex marriage. At that time, at most, six of the 47 Convention states allowed same-sex marriage. It was no longer possible to say that the right in art.12 was necessarily limited to opposite sex couples; rather, whether to allow same-sex marriage was a matter to be regulated by national law. It was not for the Court to substitute its own judgement for that of the national authority. It could not be said that art.12 required the respondent government to grant same-sex couples access to marriage. There had been no violation of art.12.

The only restriction on the right to found a family recognised by art.12 is national law. There is a wide margin of appreciation but restrictions must not affect the very essence of the right and must be proportionate; so a Court order which reflected a divorce court's assessment of an applicant's culpability in the break up of his first marriage by prohibiting his remarriage for three years was held to constitute a breach (*F v Switzerland* (1987)). However, in *R (Mellor) v Secretary of State for the Home Department* (2002), the Divisional Court held that art.12 did not entitle a prisoner to artificial insemination facilities.

PROTOCOL 1 ARTICLE 2

Article 2 of Protocol 1 provides: **13–06**

> "No person shall be denied the right to education. In the exercise of any functions which it assumes in relation to education and to teaching, the State shall respect the right of parents to ensure such

education and teaching in conformity with their own religious and philosophical convictions."

In *R (on the application of Holub) v Secretary of State for the Home Department* (2001), the Court of Appeal said that the general right to education comprises a right of access to such educational establishments as exist; a right to effective (but not the most effective possible) education; and a right to official recognition of academic qualifications. In that case, returning unsuccessful asylum seekers to Poland would not breach the right because their daughter would be able to get an effective education in Poland.

In practice, the issues have related to the right of parents to insist on particular forms of education and the case law has been concerned chiefly with the limitation of those rights.

It should be noted that the UK has made a reservation to this provision, restricting respect for parents' rights to that which is compatible with efficient instruction and the avoidance of unreasonable public expenditure. The effect of that, as a matter of international law, is to modify the Protocol to that extent as it applies to the UK.

In the case law, it has been held that parents have no right to insist on single sex or selective schools (*W and DM v United Kingdom* (1984)); and that there is no obligation on states to establish or subsidise education of any particular type (*Belgian Linguistic Case (No.2)* (1979–1980)). Exclusion of a pupil from school will not breach the article if an alternative package of education is offered (*A v Head Teacher and Governors of Lord Grey School* (2006)).

The article does apply to tertiary education but does not create a right to state funding for individual students (*R (on the application of Douglas) v North Tyneside MBC* (2004).

PROTOCOL 1 ARTICLE 3

13–07 This article provides:

"The High Contracting Parties undertake to hold free elections at reasonable intervals by secret ballot, under conditions which will ensure the free expression of the opinion of the people in the choice of the legislature."

In *Gitonas v Greece* (1986), the Court explained that that the rights thus conferred are not absolute and that states have a wide margin of appreciation in setting conditions for election provided that the conditions set do not curtail the rights to such an extent as to impair their very essence, that they are imposed in pursuit of a legitimate aim and that the means employed are not disproportionate. In that case, a rule that salaried civil servants and others, including members of staff of public law entities, may not stand for election as members of parliament in any constituency where they have performed their duties for more than three months during the three years preceding the election was held to satisfy these tests. As we have seen above, in *Hirst v United Kingdom* (2005), the Court considered that the UK's blanket prohibition on prisoners voting was disproportionate and constituted a breach of the right.

ARTICLES 16 AND 17

We mention these provisions for the sake of completeness. Article 16 **13–08** provides that nothing in arts 10, 11 and 14 shall be regarded as preventing the high contracting parties from imposing restrictions on the political activity of aliens. It tends to be interpreted rather restrictively and that tendency has been increased by the treaty on European Union and the rights which it gives to citizens of that union (*Piermont v France* (1995)).

Article 17 provides:

> "Nothing in this Convention may be interpreted as implying for any State, group or person any right to engage in any activity or perform any act aimed at the destruction of any of the rights and freedoms set for [in the Convention] or at their limitation to any greater extent than is provided for in the Convention."

On this basis, the Commission dismissed a complaint by applicants who had been prevented from standing for election on a racist platform (*Glimmerveen and Hagenbeek v the Netherlands* (1979)). In *Norwood v United Kingdom* (2004), the Court held that to display a poster attacking Muslims in seriously offensive and inflammatory terms and urging their removal from the country was an act within the meaning of art.17 and not, therefore, within the protection of the art.10 right to freedom of expression.

14. PROHIBITION OF DISCRIMINATION
(ARTICLE 14)

INTRODUCTION

14–01 Article 14 provides:

> "The enjoyment of the rights and freedoms set forth in this Convention shall be secured without any discrimination on any ground such as sex, race, colour, language, religion, political or other opinion, national or social origin, association with a national minority, property, birth or other status."

The treatment of art.14 in these final pages does not imply that it is residual or an afterthought. It is because art.14 never stands alone. In terms, it refers to discrimination as to the rights guaranteed by the Convention. It is not a free-standing prohibition on discrimination. It always and only operates in conjunction with one of the other articles. If the discrimination alleged does not relate to a right guaranteed under the Convention, art.14 does not assist the applicant.

The operation of art.14

14–02 The approach taken by the Court is usually (but not invariably) to begin by considering the substantive article. If there is a breach of that article, it does not usually find it necessary to consider art.14. If, however, there is no breach of the article, the Court will (if the issue is raised) go on to consider whether there is nevertheless discrimination in the application of the substantive right. Discrimination is a difference in treatment that does not have an objective and reasonable justification (*Thlimmenos v Greece* (2001); *Pretty v United Kingdom* (2002)).

In *St Brice v Southwark London Borough Council* (2002), the Court of Appeal held, that since a council's decision to pursue the eviction of the appellant by proceeding in the county court and obtaining a warrant of possession, rather than by proceeding in the High Court, was not based on any personal characteristic of the appellant, it could not constitute discrimination for the purposes of art.14. By contrast, in reviewing the operation of s.23 of the Anti-terrorism, Crime and Security Act 2001, which permitted detention without trial of foreign suspects but not of British ones, the House of Lords held that the provision fell foul of art.14 (*A v Secretary of State for the Home Department* (2005)).

The way this works appears may be seen from *Abdulaziz, Cabales and Balkandali v United Kingdom* (1985). In that case, the applicants were women who were lawfully settled in the UK in accordance with immigration rules in force at the time (which were a product of the transformation of the British Empire into the Commonwealth), their husbands were refused permission to remain with or join them. The applicants complained that they had been the victims of discrimination, inter alia on the ground of sex, so that there had been violations of art.8, alone or in conjunction with art.14. On the art.8 point, it was clear that there was an interference with the right to respect for family life; the applicants were being deprived of, or threatened with the deprivation of, the society of their husbands. However, states enjoy a wide margin of appreciation as regards respect for family life and art.8 does not oblige states to respect the choice of a state of residence by couples who are marrying. The applicants must all have known at the time of marrying of the limitations on their husbands' rights to be in the UK and there was therefore no breach of art.8 taken on its own. Nevertheless, it was easier for a man settled in the UK to get permission for his wife to join him than for a woman to get such permission for her husband. The advancement of equality of the sexes is a major goal in the Member States of the Council of Europe, so

> "very weighty reasons would have to be advanced before a difference in treatment on the ground of sex could be regarded as compatible with the Convention".

The Government's argument that male immigrants would have a more significant effect on the labour market than female ones was not convincing. Accordingly, although there had been no breach of art.8 in absolute terms, it was established that the UK treated requests for permission for spouses to immigrate differently according to whether the person already settled in the UK was male or female. No sufficient justification having been put forward, the Court held that there had been a breach of art.8 in conjunction with art.14.

In *Abdulaziz*, the applicants were female. *Burghartz v Switzerland* (1994) is an example of the application of art.14 where the person discriminated against was male. The applicants were a married couple who chose on marriage to use the wife's surname, "Burghartz", the husband putting his own surname before it and calling himself "Schnyder Burghartz". The Swiss authorities registered them both as "Schnyder", refusing to recognise any other formula on the basis that in Swiss law only a wife could put her surname before the family name. As a result, a large number of official documents, including the husband's certificate of his doctorate in history, did not include the "Burghartz" element. The Court, having established that art.8 is relevant to the question of a person's name, proceeded to consider arts 14 and 8 together. It found that the difference of treatment between husbands and wives complained of lacked an objective and reasonable justification and accordingly contravened art.14 taken together with art.8.

What is important about this is that the Court found it necessary, before considering the question of discrimination, to answer the first question applicable to art.8—was the right relevant to what had happened? Only then did it address the discrimination point and it did so taking arts 8 and 14 together.

Objective and reasonable justification

14–03 Finally, on art.14, we should pay some attention to the matter of objective and reasonable justification. This expression is derived from the *Belgian Linguistic Case (No.2)* (1979–1980). In *Darby v Sweden* (1991) the Court elaborated on this, saying that a difference in the treatment of individuals

> "will only be discriminatory if it 'has no objective and reasonable justification', that is if it does not pursue a 'legitimate aim' and if there is no 'reasonable relationship of proportionality between the means employed and the aim sought to be realised'".

When one recalls that art.14 operates in conjunction with the other Convention rights, as to which legitimate aim and proportionality are essential criteria for establishing whether an interference with the right is permissible, it is understandable that the Court should have wished to analyse art.14 questions in these terms; and they represent for us, at the very end of the book, territory which should be thoroughly familiar.

INDEX